METAL CRAFT

LINDA & OPIE O'BRIEN

DISCOVERY WORKSHOP

CREATE UNIQUE JEWELRY, ART DOLLS, COLLAGE ART, KEEPSAKES AND MORE!

NORTH LIGHT BOOKS
CINCINNATI, OHIO
WWW.ARTISTSNETWORK.COM

METRIC CONVERSION CHART

To convert	to	multiply by
Inches	Centimeters	2.54
Centimeters	Inches	0.4
Feet	Centimeters	30.5
Centimeters	Feet	0.03
Yards	Meters	0.9
Meters	Yards	1.1
Sq. Inches	Sq. Centimeters	6.45
Sq. Centimeters	Sq. Inches	0.16
Sq. Feet	Sq. Meters	0.09
Sq. Meters	Sq. Feet	10.8
Sq. Yards	Sq. Meters	0.8
Sq. Meters	Sq. Yards	1.2
Pounds	Kilograms	0.45
Kilograms	Pounds	2.2
Ounces	Grams	28.3
Grams	Ounces	0.035

09 08 07 06 05   5 4 3 2 1

Distributed in Canada by Fraser Direct
100 Armstrong Avenue
Georgetown, ON, Canada L7G 5S4
Tel: (905) 877-4411

Distributed in the U.K. and Europe by David & Charles
Brunel House, Newton Abbot, Devon, TQ12 4PU, England
Tel: (+44) 1626 323200, Fax: (+44) 1626 323319
Email: mail@davidandcharles.co.uk

Distributed in Australia by Capricorn Link
P.O. Box 704, S. Windsor, NSW 2756 Australia
Tel: (02) 4577-3555

Library of Congress Cataloging-in-Publication Data
O'Brien, Linda, Metal craft discovery workshop: create unique jewelry, art dolls, collage art, keepsakes and more! / Linda and Opie O'Brien.
   p. cm.
  Includes index.
  ISBN 1-58180-646-9 (pbk. : alk. paper)
  1. Metal-work. I. O'Brien, Opie, II. Title.
  TT205.0245 2005
  745.56--dc22   2005008499

Editor: Tonia Davenport
Cover Designer: Karla Baker
Interior Designer: Davis Stanard
Production Coordinator: Jennifer Wagner
Cover Photographer: Al Parrish
Interior Photographers: Dina Rossi, Tim Grondin
Photo Stylist: Jan Nickum

About the Authors

Linda and Opie O'Brien are full-time mixed media artists who enjoy pushing the envelope through their imaginative use of metal, organic, recycled and found materials. Their work, which includes jewelry, books, assemblage, collage, dolls, masks and more, has been featured in numerous books, magazines, galleries, group and solo shows, museum gift shops and private collections.

Opie, an artist and musician, attended the School of Visual Arts and also studied at Pratt Institute in New York City. On the musical side of the coin, he played Carnegie Hall and Madison Square Garden with the Raspberries and Tommy James. His approach to art is disciplined, structured and meticulous.

Linda, on the other hand, is self-taught. Her philosophy is "no rules, no restrictions." Her raw, free-spirited style and nontraditional techniques, define her as a true "outsider" artist. She has written feature articles for several publications including *Belle Armoire* and *Art Doll Quarterly* magazines.

New York transplants who enjoy living on Lake Erie in Northeast Ohio, with their cat Angelus and his cat Angel, Linda and Opie own Burnt Offerings Studio and enjoy teaching art workshops nationally and in Mexico.

Visit their Web site at www.burntofferings.com.

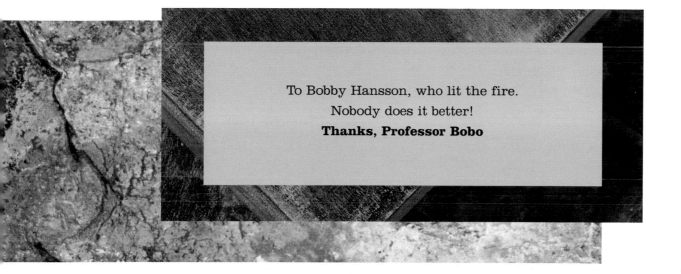

To Bobby Hansson, who lit the fire.
Nobody does it better!
Thanks, Professor Bobo

Acknowledgments

We'd like to express thanks to the following people who helped bring this book to fruition: to North Light Books and Tricia Waddell for giving us this opportunity; to MaryJo McGraw for suggesting that it be on metal; and to Sharilyn Miller for opening so many doors. To Dina Rossi, our photographer and close friend for over 10 years, for always capturing our best side and never complaining, even when we needed something "yesterday". . . so far, this has been our best adventure! To Tim Grondin, the photographer; Karla Baker, the designer; and Jan Nickum, the photo stylist at North Light, for the cover, beauty shots and finishing touches. To our students and friends for inspiring us to always be our best creative selves. To our family for their never ending encouragement, belief and support (emphasis on support), and to Ruth for making Opie's funky hat.

To my Aunt Fran, who continues to watch over me, you are greatly missed . . . and last but not least, to Tonia Davenport, our editor extraordinaire who kept us on track and exemplifies the phrase "multi-tasking," you've been a wellspring of ingenious ideas, creative solutions and continuous smiles.

CONTENTS

introDUCTION

* Metal is an exciting material. Whether it's shiny and new or old and worn, it has a presence few can resist. Since 1994, we have been working with various types of metal and combining it with a myriad of mixed media. In fact, pairing metal with organic, recycled and found materials has become our passion.

Over the years we've learned from our mistakes and we've also made many wonderful discoveries that we're very excited to share with you. We call our process "metalcrafting *our* way": a stress free, nontraditional approach to a time-honored discipline.

Think of this book as a journey, and as with any journey, there are many paths that can lead to the final destination. Our intention is to lead you down the path of least resistance; our hope is to simplify and demystify the process; and our desire is to assist you in finding your own creative voice as you soar to new artistic heights.

Basically, this book will begin with an extensive getting-started section and then follow with three chapters of projects. The techniques in the first section will serve as a reference guide that you can keep coming back to, as often as you need. It explains all of the different techniques you will need to know to complete the projects, as well as explores many different options available, so that when you're ready to construct your pieces you will be able to make choices based on your own personal preferences.

We'll start with some fundamentals: cutting, drilling and punching metal, creating windows in metal without using a jeweler's saw and deconstructing a tin can. From there we'll move on to our favorite attachment techniques, known as cold connections. Then on to metal etching, patinas, oxidizing and aging, as well as some image transfer techniques that really complement metal. We'll conclude with several methods for texturing metal, embossing metal foil and finally, combining resins with metal.

After learning the basics, you'll explore numerous projects, which will include jewelry, journals, dolls, wall art pieces, assemblage art and more. While they are presented as step-by-step projects, you'll find you will always have options available to you, such as whether or not to add a patina, to oxidize your metal, to transfer an image or to etch your piece. This will be an exciting adventure, so let's begin!

tools and MATERIALS

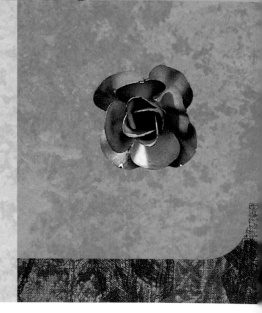

✳ "The right tool for the right job!" We've all heard that before and to a large extent it's true, but as individuals, we have different preferences. I'm more of a hand tool person, while Opie's credo is "more power." Most of the time, either philosophy will get the job done (however, it's worth remembering there's an exception to every rule).

We've listed several items in each category. You'll be introduced to a variety of metals, wire, hammers, drills, punches, snips, shears, and so on. We've even included a miscellaneous category. When viewing the following lists, understand that you will not need all of them, you probably already have many of them and, you'll find as you work with metal, you'll come to rely on just a few of them.

METAL

In no time at all, you'll be cutting metal as easily as if it were paper. But before you learn how to cut it, you must first know where to find it and learn a bit about its different gauges and the types that are available.

Metal foils are the thinnest of the metals we'll be using and they are very pliable (think of aluminum foil). They are great for any type of embossing. Foils come in different colors and can be found in craft and stamp stores as well as online.

Metal also comes in a sheet form, which is thicker than foil and, depending on the type you want, can be found in craft and hardware stores, hobby shops and online. Detail-cutting tin shears can comfortably cut sheet metal up to 18-gauge. Copper, brass and tin sheet are both economical and easy to find. Ster-

ling silver is more expensive and usually used for jewelry. It must be purchased from a jewelry supply store.

Metal mesh is a material that almost resembles fabric, and you can do some truly amazing things with it.

Then . . . there's the tin can, an almost perfect metal as, oftentimes, it's free! It's found almost everywhere from grocery stores to garage sales and can always be recycled into something wonderful. Not to mention, you end up with a unique conversation piece to boot!

No matter how you look at it, metal is a fantastic material. It's exciting and seductive. It can be altered, aged, weathered with a patina, encased, embossed, have images transferred onto it and sometimes even sewn. Are you ready?

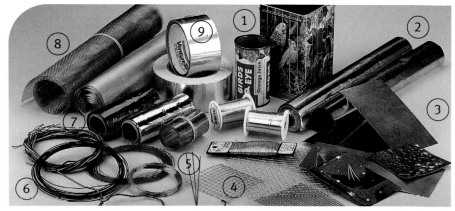

The metals we'll be working with:

1. tin cans
2. metal foil
3. sheet metal
4. hardware cloth and screen
5. metal rods
6. variety of wire
7. more metal foil
8. copper and brass mesh
9. metal tape

PILES OF FILES

Assorted files and sanding materials are used to smooth the edges of metal, as well as give it a tooth or texture. Because your projects and pieces of metal will vary in size, it's a good idea to have a variety of files at your work station to accommodate intricate as well as large-surface areas. Some of the tools shown here are used to mark metal when making measurements.

1. 12" (31cm) square with scribe
2. steel wool
3. sanding block, pad and papers
4. awls
5. metal files in a variety of shapes and sizes
6. rulers
7. vise

1. dremel and drill press
2. anvil
3. steel block and machinist's square
4. electric and hand drills
5. pop rivet gun
6. nibbler
7. paper punches
8. center punches
9. handheld eyelet and grommet setters
10. metal stamps and chisels
11. glass cutter (for scoring metal)
12. needle tool
13. large hand punch
14. two-hole metal punch
15. can opener
16. two American tag eyelet setters and punch machine (one is a handheld unit)
17. assortment of drill bits

DRILLS AND PUNCHES

These are the tools that make holes in metal. Sometimes holes can be decorative, but most often, you will be making holes in order to attach something to your piece or to connect two pieces of metal together. Using hand punches makes quick work of hole-making, but sometimes you need a hole where a punch will not reach; enter the drill. Drills and a variety of drill bits can serve nearly all of your hole-making needs. Look for bits that are made for metal. While the ones for wood will often work, they may dull more quickly.

SNIPS, SHEARS AND PLIERS

Cutting metal is no hassle at all when you have the right tools. There are several shown here. We use both heavy-duty tin snips and detail-cutting shears to deconstruct the rims and seams on tin cans. Decorative scissors can be used for cutting foils. The large yellow-handled heavy-duty end cutters are great for cutting metal coat hangers and heavy gauge wire.The red-handled cable cutter cleanly cuts hard wire like music or spring wire. In addition to cutting heavier wire, we use the cable cutter to cut nails to size when we make rivets.

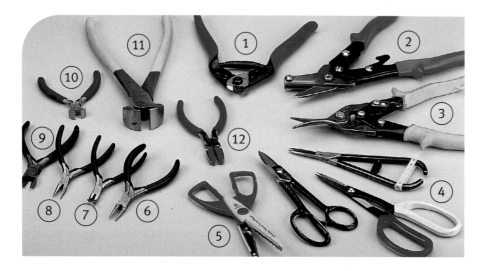

1. cable cutters
2. heavy-duty nibbler (also known as a double-cut pipe cutter)
3. aviation snips
4. three detail-cutting tin shears
5. decorative scissors
6. round nose pliers
7. bent nose pliers
8. chain nose pliers
9. flush cutters
10. fine end cutters
11. heavy-duty end cutters
12. plastic-jawed straightening pliers

HAMMERS AND MALLETS

Hammers and mallets are among our favorite tools. A striking hammer works best when using metal stamps, a chasing hammer flattens metal and a rubber mallet flattens metal, but will not scratch the surface. The other specialty hammers shown here each serve a specific need, but it's not mandatory that you have them all. Finally, striking surfaces are a must. Steel, wood and rubber surfaces all have their place and you will want to have one of each.

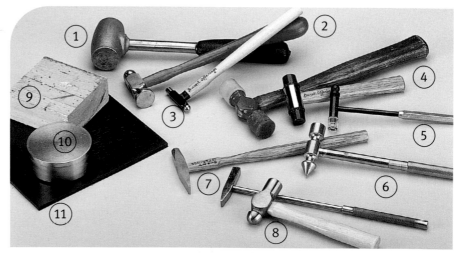

1. large brass striking hammer
2. chasing hammer
3. rivet hammer
4. two rubber mallet-hammers
5. interchangeable-heads hammer
6. brass hammer
7. two cross peen hammers
8. eyelet-setting hammer
9. wood block
10. metal block
11. hard rubber mat

ODDS AND ENDS

This can also be called the good and plenty category (it's plenty full of good stuff). These are the items that you will use to add finishing touches and unique details to your metal projects. Paper crimpers and tube wringers give metal foil and metal sheet a crinkle-cut texture; rubber stamps and ink allow you to add text or other imagery; a mini torch gives copper and brass a beautiful patina; and a bone folder or stylus lets you emboss metal foil. Along with these tools are some less glamorous supplies like adhesives and a jar of spackle, but don't underestimate the necessity of these common materials.

1. pasta machine
2. paper crimper
3. vise grip
4. metal tube wringer
5. heat gun
6. gloves
7. rubber stamps and ink
8. craft knife
9. permanent markers
10. butane lighter
11. mini quilt iron
12. tacking iron
13. eye protection
14. mini torch and butane
15. Dorlands wax
16. brayer
17. craft stick, half of a bone folder
18. paintbrush
19. assortment of adhesives including liquid glue, a glue stick, gel medium, E-6000, and masking tape
20. spackle
21. mini metal bending brake
22. wire bender

basic METAL TECHNIQUES

* Just as a journey begins with a single step, crafting metal usually begins with a single cut. By following a few simple rules, you'll soon master this technique and the many others that we'll discuss in this section of the book. Metal is a very easy material to work with—really!

Clockwise from twelve o'clock: a ruler, detail-cutting shears, file, linoleum block and rubber mallet, permanent marker, tin can fragments and rubbing alcohol.

SNIPS OR SHEARS?

Some people refer to snips as shears and vice versa. In this book we will always refer to tin snips when heavy-duty snips are warranted and tin shears when fine or detail cutting is needed.

CUTTING SHAPES FROM A METAL SHEET

The thickness or gauge of metal usually determines the tool necessary for cutting it. All of the projects in this book will use metal that is 18-gauge or thinner and can be easily cut with tin shears, sometimes called fine or detail shears. The exception to this are the rims and seams found on tin cans, which require heavy-duty tin snips (see Deconstructing a Tin Can, page 14).

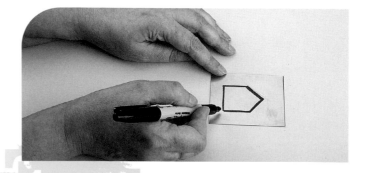

Draw your Design
Draw your design with a permanent marker.

2   Take Small Cuts

Holding the metal in one hand, take very small, counter-clockwise cuts, being mindful to never let the blades of your shears touch. This helps avoid burrs and sharp edges. Turn the metal into the blade as you cut. If you're cutting with your left hand, do this in reverse and cut clockwise.

3   Remove Excess Metal

Sometimes you reach a place where you can just rough-cut away the unwanted area, instead of twisting your wrist into an uncomfortable or unnatural position. Once the excess is removed, you can continue cutting counterclockwise.

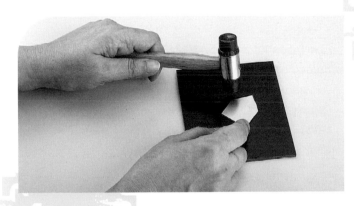

4   Flatten

Place the metal on a hard pounding surface and flatten the edges using your rubber mallet. This usually removes the rough and/or sharp edges.

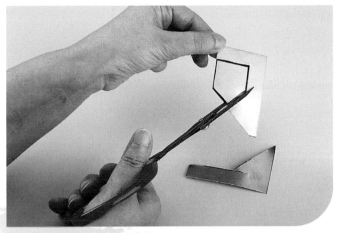

5   File

Use a metal file to remove any remaining sharp edges. Always file in one direction and away from you.

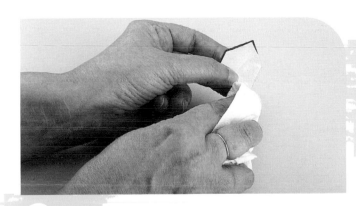

6   Clean

Remove all permanent marker marks, with ordinary rubbing alcohol, using a soft cloth or paper towel.

DECONSTRUCTING A TIN CAN

Breathing new life into a discarded item destined for the scrap heap really makes you feel good, and tin cans are a wonderful material to work with. Readily available from garage sales, thrift stores, the supermarket or friends and family, tin cans and canisters can easily be taken apart and prepared for the making of art with just a can opener and heavy-duty tin snips.

Can opener, tin canister, heavy-duty tin snips and a rubber mallet.

1 Remove the Bottom
Remove the bottom of the canister with a can opener. If you are deconstructing a regular can, also remove the top.

OPEN WIDE . . .

Note that all rims are not created equal and may vary in thickness. You will have the most success with a can opener that opens to 180°.

2 Snip Out a Section of the Lid
When you have a removable lid, as in candy or cookie tins, make two cuts in the rim of the lid, about 1" (3cm) apart, with your snips. Bend it up until it is flush with the top of the lid and then cut it off.

3 Cut the Lid's Side Portion Away

Insert your snips into that opening and then cut the side portion off.

4 Cut Both Rims

Once the top and bottom of the can or canister are removed, you'll notice there is a thin rim on both ends of the can. Using only the tip of your tin snips, cut both rims at the seam. The rims could also be cut with heavy duty wire cutters.

5 Cut the Seam

With your tin snips, cut halfway down the length of the seam.

6 Turn the Can Over

Turn the can over and repeat from the other end until the seam is completely cut. This is much easier than making one continuous cut, particularly on a larger can.

7 Remove the Seam

With your snips cutting right next to the seam, remove it.

8 Remove the First Rim

Cut around the perimeter of the can, using your snips, and remove the first rim.

9 Remove the Other Rim

Turn the canister over and repeat, removing the second rim.

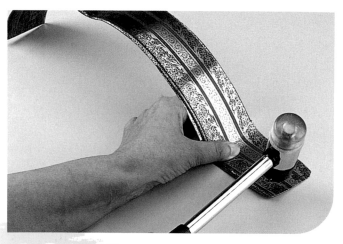

10 Flatten the Can

Using a rubber mallet and working in small sections, flatten the can. The rubber mallet also works well for dulling burrs and sharp edges. You now have a piece of metal that is ready to be transformed into art.

REMOVING THE EXCESS

To make life easier when removing the rims, at the halfway point, remove the portion of the rim that has been cut, using only the tip of your snips. This gets it out of your way.

CREATING WINDOWS IN METAL

Sounds impossible? Well it's really quite simple. Several years ago, I came to the realization that I was jewelers' saw-impaired! However, my love of beautiful imagery peering through mysterious windows in both our metal jewelry and smaller projects prompted this cool discovery that requires minimal tools and even less effort!

From twelve o'clock: a drill, wood block, center punch, hammer, nibbler, metal file, hand punch with dies and goggles.

1 Select and Mark Your Metal

Using a permanent marker, draw an area to be cut out. You can use a template or a ruler for accuracy.

2 Make a Hole or Two

With a drill and a ⅜" (10mm) bit, or a punch and a ⁹⁄₃₂" (7mm) die, make a hole or two inside the drawn line that is wide enough to insert the head of the nibbler. (One hole is needed with the drill and two overlapping holes are needed if using the punch.) For more on drilling, see Drilling and Punching Metal, page 18.

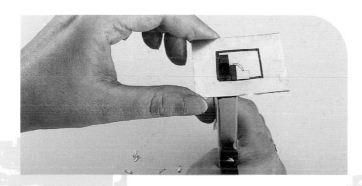

3 Insert the Nibbler

Put the head of the tool into the hole and just nibble your way through the metal by squeezing the handle. When you get to the corners, reposition the head of the tool as needed. With a little practice, you'll soon be a pro. Jewelers' saw begone!

4 File the Edges

Insert your metal file into the opening and file until smooth.

DRILLING AND PUNCHING METAL

Making holes in metal gives us the freedom to join layers together, add embellishments or jewelry findings, hang things and much more.

From twelve o'clock: a hand drill, rotary drill, hand punch, two-hole metal punch, hammer, wood block, center punch, permanent marker and goggles

Punching

My favorite tool by far is my two-hole metal punch that punches perfect $\frac{1}{16}$" (1.6mm) and $\frac{3}{32}$" (2.3mm) holes. I use it exclusively for all of my jewelry work. A hand punch set with changeable heads ranging from $\frac{3}{32}$" (2.3mm) all the way up to $\frac{9}{32}$" (7mm) seems to serve the rest of my needs. The wide mouth of the punch allows for deeper access into interior areas.

Drilling

A rotary drill with a flexible shaft has many attachments that also allow you to cut, sand, polish and more. Opie is a rotary drill kind of guy! I prefer a quiet hand drill complete with various sizes of drill bits.

Ink Marks the Spot

With a permanent marker, mark where you want the hole and use a manual two-hole punch to punch it out. You don't need a nail or center punch.

X Marks the Spot

Working on a wood block, first make an indent in the spot where you want the hole to be with either a hammer and nail or a center punch. Without this indent, the drill bit will move and scratch the metal. The technical term for this disaster is *walking*.

Drill

Still working on a wood block, place the bit of an electric drill on the indentation and drill the hole.

MAKING COLD CONNECTIONS (RIVETS, WIRE AND SCREWS—OH MY!)

Securing two pieces of metal together is called making a connection and there are two kinds: hot and cold. Hot connections require solder and heat from a torch or a soldering iron. All of the projects in this book will incorporate a variety of cold connections that require no heat and are a great way to engage your creativity because of the numerous options available. Rivets, eyelets, screws, wire, glue and even fiber are all examples of cold connections. As the latter two are self-explanatory, we will focus on our favorite cold connections: pop rivets, nail rivets and eyelets, as well as screws and wire. No matter which type of rivet you choose, you need to make a hole in both pieces of metal to connect them.

From twelve o'clock: a rotary drill, pop rivet gun, hand drill, two-hole metal punch, rivet hammer, center punch, end cutters, chain-nose pliers, flush cutters and round-nose pliers, wood and metal blocks, wire, hand punch, and in the center, pop rivets and nails.

Pop Rivets

Pop rivets load into a pop rivet gun and are available from any hardware store. Each package comes with complete directions. The ⅛" (3mm) aluminum rivets are the most popular and the easiest to work with. Copper is the most expensive and most difficult to work with (but it looks great). Opie is very partial to pop rivets and we use them in most tin can doll constructions, especially at the neck, because of their strength.

1 Make a Hole

Punch or drill a ⅛" (3mm) hole in both pieces of metal to be joined.

2 Insert the Rivet

Insert a rivet through the holes, from the front of the piece until the rim rests on the metal, with the stem pointing up. (The stem must be pointing up.)

3 Position the Gun

Load the stem into the gun until the tip is firmly pressed against the rivet.

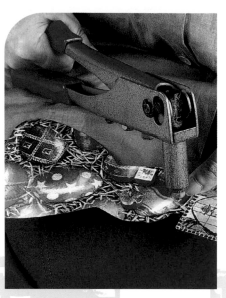

4 Use Your Own Body Language

Rest the bottom handle of the rivet gun on your thigh.

5 Squeeze the Handle

While firmly holding the two pieces of metal in one hand, squeeze the handle all the way before you ease up, then slowly release the handle and squeeze again (it might take a few squeezes before the rivet pops). You will be able to feel when the rivet has popped.

6 Pop Goes the Rivet

The rivet has popped and, as you can see, her head is now firmly on her shoulders.

Eyelets

These are the easiest of all rivets; they are kind of like instant gratification rivets. They are available everywhere and come in a variety of sizes, colors and styles. We will use eyelets to attach the bottlecap wings to the watch dial body.

1 Drill or Punch Holes

Mark where you want the eyelets to go and drill or punch the holes in both pieces of metal.

2 Insert and Set

Working on a metal block, put the eyelet in the holes and set it with the eyelet setter by hitting it with a hammer. One good strike is often all you need.

Nail Rivets

As the name suggests, this type of rivet is made from an ordinary nail. Nails come in copper, silver, brass and sometimes black. They give a beautiful hand-finished look to jewelry and smaller projects because one side of the rivet already has a finished nail head. The nails best suited for this are between 17- and 19-gauge and ½" to ¾" (13mm to 19mm) long. They fit perfectly into a ¹⁄₁₆" (1.6mm) hole. When using nails to create rivets, always work on a steel block.

Insert the Nail and Snip

Place a nail through the holes in both pieces of the metal. (The nailhead should be on the front, but turn the piece over, as you'll be creating your rivet from the back side.) With end-cut pliers, snip off the excess nail, leaving only a very tiny piece exposed above the metal. If you leave too much of the nail, it will bend as you create your rivet instead of flaring or mushrooming out, and you will have to start again with a new nail.

Hammer

Using a rivet hammer (we find that a 1- or 2-oz. hammer works best for this) and a light tapping motion—do not hold the hammer in a death grip (relaxed and easy-does-it here)—tap around the outer edges of the nail in a circular motion until the nail starts to flare out. This may take awhile in the beginning until you become comfortable with the process, but soon it will become second nature and a favorite way to connect things.

Screws

The last items we will be adding to our piece are a vintage bone game piece and a couple of boots. The bone is too fragile for hammering a rivet or eyelet, so we'll solve this problem by using tiny screws, washers and nuts.

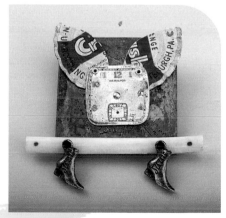

Insert the Screws

From the front, insert a screw into a hole in one boot, and then set a washer on the screw. Insert the screw through the hole in the bone, and then through the copper piece. Add one nut to the back, and then repeat with the other screw, washer and nut in the other hole.

Now We are Complete!

Here is our finished piece, viewed from the front. All this piece needs now is the addition of a pendant attachment (which we'll cover later) and it is ready to wear!

Wire

Sometimes, an interesting wire wrap will become your only means of joinery. Personally, we try to combine as many cold connections as possible into any given piece, just because of the aesthetics they provide.

This wire-wrap method works especially well as a means of cold-connecting. We have great success using between 16-gauge (thickest) and 20-gauge (thinnest) wire. We will use a tin can doll as our demo piece and will accomplish two tasks in just one step. We will make a wire loop hanger (without having to solder) so we can display our doll on a wall, and at the same time, attach vintage game pieces to her chest. We have come to call this method the Torpedo Wrap.

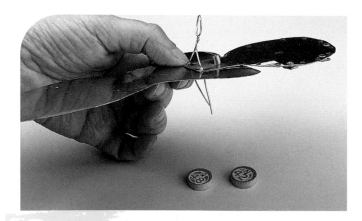

1 Create a Loop
Make a loop and hold it securely with your pliers as you twist it about three times with your other hand.

2 Punch Your Holes
Using an awl, place your doll on either a wood block or an old phone book and punch two holes big enough to accommodate the wire.

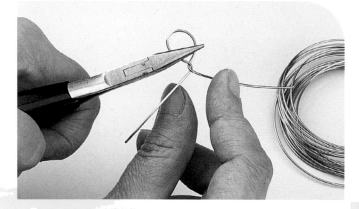

3 Insert the Wire
With the loop to the back, insert the wire into the holes and trim the ends to about 1" (3cm) or so.

4 Twist
On the front of the doll, add the game pieces onto the wire (you will need to have drilled a hole in them first). Using just the tip of your round-nose pliers, make a small loop and, with half-turns of your wrist, continue until you've made three spiral loops, tight and close together to secure the pieces.

ETCHING METAL

This is one of our very favorite techniques because it takes a plain piece of copper or brass and creates a permanent design, forever etched into the surface, using either ordinary rubber stamps or, if you wish to create your own custom design, any permanent marking pen. Always start with clean metal that has been cut to your desired shape with tin shears and sanded in a circular motion to give the metal a tooth. This improves the etch, so don't be shy—put a little elbow grease into it!

A word about PCB etchant solution. It is a solution that contains ferric chloride and was designed to etch PC boards. It should be used full strength, not diluted with water. We prefer Radio Shack's version over other brands, because it is safe to flush when you are finished with it. You may want to wear rubber gloves whenever you work with PCB, because it can stain your hands.

From the left: tweezers or tongs, a lidded container for the solution, permanent black ink pad, masking tape, PCB etchant solution, rubber stamps (bold graphics work best), permanent marking pen, .025 copper or brass sheet from craft, hardware or hobby shops.

1 — To Stamp or To Draw...

Either rubber stamp or draw a design onto the metal with a permanent marker and set it aside to thoroughly dry.

PUT AN END TO IT

Metal continues to etch, even after you have rinsed it in water. To completely stop the process, submerge the piece in a 50/50 ratio of ammonia and water.

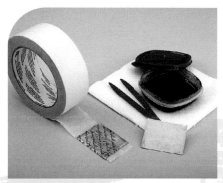

2 — Into the Etch

After it has dried, protect the back side with masking tape. Submerge the piece in enough solution to cover it, being careful not to overlap multiple pieces. Put the lid on it and set it aside. Check your results every hour or so. The longer you keep the metal in the solution, the deeper the etch. You're finished only when the results are pleasing to you. Experiment and play with the process, after all . . . it's not as if these rules were etched in stone!

3 — Scrub-A-Dub-Dub

When you're happy with the results, take the pieces out of the etch using either plastic or copper tweezers, discard the backing tape and rinse well. Using a kitchen scrubbie pad, sand off all of the remaining ink (or not, it's entirely your choice) . . . but by doing this step, you can really highlight and bring out the etching process.

At this point, you will still have several other options open to you, like adding a patina or aging and oxidizing your metal further, using the techniques that we will cover next.

AGING METAL

In many instances, shiny metal just isn't desired and you will want to give your piece an aged look. There are several options available to you, which include techniques that will darken the metal by using either oxidizing or aging products, such as liver of sulfur. If you're looking for beautiful greens, blues and rusts, you can use a patina. There are commercial patina kits available from your local craft store such as the ones from Modern Options, but our focus here will be on the three patinas that we use most often, which you can easily create at home. These patinas are safe, simple and fun, and use simple products that you probably already have on hand. The satisfaction you'll get from creating these patinas from scratch will be immeasurable (and, in one particular case, you might even say . . . delicious!).

SEEING DOUBLE?

When using metal stamps, the goal is to strike the stamp only once or you may have a double imprint on your metal piece. As usual, practice makes perfect.

Oxidizing With Liver of Sulfur

Liver of sulfer comes in both liquid or crystal form and has exact mixing directions on the package. We use it a lot to darken metal, especially metal that we've first stamped words into. You will get better results if the metal is heated on a hot plate, and as far as hot plates go, cup and candle warmers work really well for this. For larger projects requiring submersion, use very warm water when you mix your solution, instead of heating the metal with a hot plate.

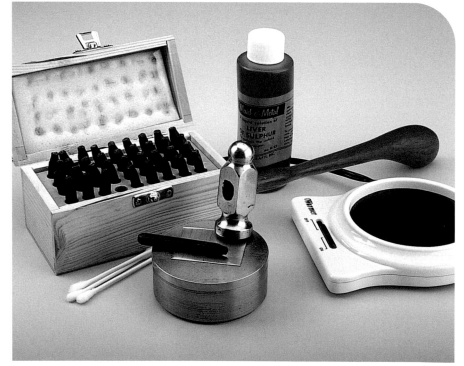

Liver of sulfur, a small hot plate, a metal block, a hammer, cotton swabs, and a metal alphabet/number stamps set.

1 Stamp It

With your piece of metal sitting on a metal block, place the first metal stamp on the copper, being mindful to hold the stamp in a vertical position, and strike it hard with your hammer. Repeat until you have spelled out your entire word. It helps to mark the metal with tiny dots to guide you where to place the stamp and to keep everything lined up nicely.

2 Heat it Up

After it's stamped, place the piece on the hot plate. Once the metal has warmed up a bit, apply the solution of liver of sulfur sparingly, using a cotton swab. You will see the metal darken instantly. Rinse your piece well, and you're done.

Aging With a Mini Torch

Wire mesh is made from copper or brass and is a wonderful material. If metal could become a fabric, this would be it. It's extremely pliable, easy to cut and, while you can use a heat gun, the absolute best way to age it is with a mini torch. The results are beautiful.

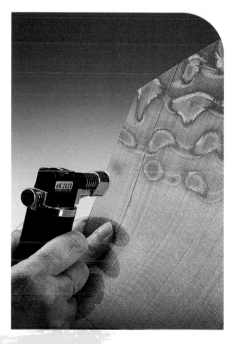

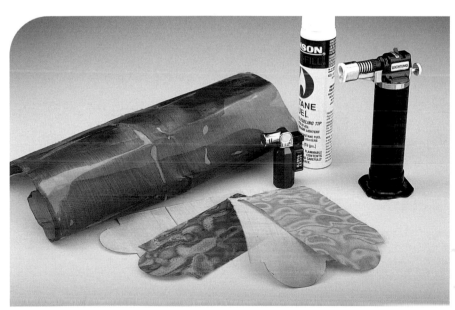

Butane, torch, copper and wire mesh

Fire Away

Hold the metal in one hand (you may wish to wear a glove for protection) and quickly move the torch over the metal in a continuous back and forth motion. You will soon see beautiful patterns appear in the metal, made from the torch. *Voilá!*

Scrumptious Patina Recipes

The following recipes are used to create beautiful patinas on copper and brass, and no matter what method you choose, all will have three things in common, so we will address those things now.

Getting started

The first step to creating any patina is to start with clean metal that has been sanded. Sanding gives the surface a tooth, which we believe has an effect on how well the patina will "stick" to the metal. Dip your piece in warm, salty water before you place it into your chosen recipe. Two of the methods that follow are submersion techniques and the other "floats" on top of a rack, as if it was being steamed. You will want to keep marked, dedicated plastic containers with lids to use over and over again for all of these processes.

Is it done yet?

How do we address "doneness"? Simply stated, the longer the metal sits in the solution and the longer it air dries, the better the patina! Ideally, it will sit in the solution overnight. That said, you can check your results after four hours. Wait longer if necessary, until you're satisfied with the results. Then lightly brush off all of the unwanted residue and leave it out to air dry.

Signed, sealed and delivered

We seal all of our pieces (usually a couple of times) with either a spray or brush-on acrylic sealer. This step eliminates the possibility of the patina flaking off. Matte or glossy is your own personal choice. If you're signing a metal piece, a permanent marker works well (we seal once, sign, then continue to seal), or you can use metal stamps and hand-hammer a signature.

Sawdust and Vinegar Recipe

This is a submersion method that produces gorgeous green hues.

BED IN A BAG

If you don't have your own wood shop or chipper, pine shavings can easily be purchased in a bag as bedding and litter in pet sections everywhere. We've tried different types of sawdust, and while most will work, pine is what actually works best for us.

Bury Your Pieces

Fill a plastic container (that has a lid), about halfway with pine shavings and completely dampen it with white distilled vinegar. Mix it well with your hand, as if you were mixing a meatloaf. The keyword here is damp; you do not want it too wet or too dry. After dipping your cleaned and sanded pieces in salty water, bury them completely in the sawdust, then put the lid on and leave it. This photo also shows what your pieces might look like when they are done.

Float Pieces Above Ammonia

Once again, start with clean, sanded metal that has been dipped in a saltwater solution. Place your pieces side by side on your rack or screen. Randomly sprinkle dry salt over each piece. Set this aside for a minute and fill the smaller container halfway with ammonia, then set that container inside the larger container. Place the screen with the salted copper pieces on top of the ammonia-filled container (you can really smell the ammonia now, so work quickly), then put the lid on the larger container and leave it.

Ammonia and Salt Recipe

This is the "floating" method and the most smelly, but if you're looking for really beautiful blues, then this is the way to get them. It calls for two lidded containers—one small, one large—a rack or screen (anything that has holes in it) to lay your pieces on, ammonia and salt (regular or seasalt or combinations of both).

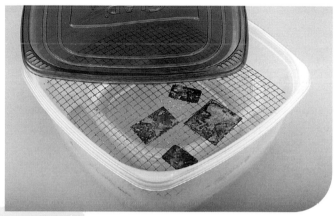

Check for "Doneness"

The salt seems to create a veining effect that looks really cool. This photo shows the beautiful blues that you'll achieve.

The Potato Chip Patina Recipe

This submersion patina is way too much fun. You'll need a spray bottle of water, a bag of salt-and-vinegar potato chips and a bowl. (Two bowls if you're planning on eating some yourself or three bowls if you're having dip as well.) As always, start with clean, sanded metal that has been dipped in salty water.

Spray With Water

Submerge the copper pieces in the bowl of potato chips (crush them up a little), and spray them well with water. Cover the bowl with a lid or plastic wrap and leave it.

Getting Hungry?

When you just can't wait any longer, check the progress of your patina. This last photo shows the end result . . . pass the dip, please!

ADDING METAL ENHANCERS

Here are some thoughts and tips on how, when, where and why we sometimes use metal paints, Copic markers and antiquing kits. All of these mediums are used to enhance the metal, but never to cover it altogether.

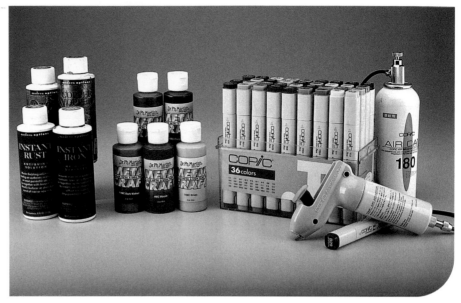

Antiquing and patina kits, metal paints, Copic markers and their airbrush attachments.

Metal Paints

Dr. Ph. Martins metal paints can be used to further enhance and/or highlight a work that's already in progress (we do not use either on just raw metal, as there would be no tooth). We use these products sparingly, a brush stroke here, a spray there, and the end results are stunning! Dr. Ph. Martins metal paints also come in a variety of colors and are simply the very best we've ever used in our never-ending quest for successfully marrying paint to metal. Never an easy feat.

Copic Markers

A fantastic product, Copic markers are not only available in over 300 colors but are also refillable. Because these pigments are alcohol-based, if you choose to use them you should definitely seal your finished piece. As markers, they are the greatest, but what we love most about Copics is how easily they convert to an airbrush system with easy-to-use air cans (so a compressor isn't even necessary). While they weren't designed for metal per se, they really do enhance metal mesh, adding subtle nuances that you couldn't get from any other medium.

Project using a patina kit on wood.

METAL CRAFT DISCOVERY WORKSHOP

Antiquing Kits

Also known as rust and/or patina kits, these materials are readily available from your craft store and even some hardware stores. They come with easy-to-follow package directions, and we've had wonderful results with these kits. The durable, aged surfaces work well with collage and are the perfect substrate for the transfer of inkjet images using gel medium (see Making Image Transfers, page 30). Combining transfers with the use of a patina kit works especially well when creating altered metal art like artist trading cards (see the ATC project on page 100), which usually involves lots of surface manipulations and multiple layers.

Antiquing kits not only provide instant rust; they also provide instant gratification when you want a patina and want it now—after all, sometimes you just can't wait! One of our most favorite things to do with these kits, however, is to combine the various patinas and create custom finishes. After a little experimentation of your own, you'll soon have people asking you how you've achieved that richly-patinated finish. These wonderful kits can be used on any surface, not just metal, allowing you complete creative freedom with no restrictions. Feel free to combine any medium with your metal. After you've used them once, we're sure you'll always have some on hand for future projects!

Project using a patina kit on metal.

MAKING IMAGE TRANSFERS

Historically, metal hasn't been the easiest surface to transfer images onto . . . but fortunately for us, this has been a decade of artistic breakthroughs, strides and discoveries that now make image transfer not only possible but easy. We will focus on two techniques: the first uses a transfer medium called Omni Gel (an all-in-one transfer, adhesive and sealer product developed by the very talented multimedia artist Beckah Krahula, who is also our very close and treasured friend). The second uses a waterslide decal. We prefer Lazertran, which, in actuality, is so much more than just a slide decal. When pairing these products with metal, you've got a match made in heaven!

From top right: laser images, heat gun, Omni Gel, tray, foam brushes, waffle-weave cloth, squeegees, trivet, tack iron, Lazertran and Lazertran images

Transfer Medium: The Basic Method

When we work with Omni Gel, we use *laser* images and *not inkjet*. Theoretically, it has been said that there are ways to get inkjet copies to work, but I truly believe in order to accomplish this, there must be perfect planetary alignment (or a precise ratio of atmospheric gases to precipitation . . . or something) because all of our bizillion attempts at success have failed. You can work with only a single image or you can gel an entire sheet of images and put the rest away for use later on. We've used images from sheets that were gelled a year ago without a hitch. Excellent directions are printed on the bottle, but we've picked up some tips and tricks along the way that we'd like to share with you. It's worth mentioning here and now that because the image will be transparent you can use either side of the sheets. One side will be kind of matte, the other kind of glossy, so even if your images have words on them, you don't have to make a reverse copy for it to work; you just need to be mindful of its placement. Once you've chosen and sized your images and had your laser copies made, you are ready to begin.

1 Brush, 1, 2, 3 . . .

Begin by applying the medium to your images, using a foam brush. Give the images a total of three coats: horizontal, vertical and diagonal. The important thing here is to apply even coats and let each coat dry completely before going on to the next one.

2 Cut and Soak

Trim the image you want to use to size, and place it in a container with very warm water. Cover it and let it soak for five minutes or so.

3 Remove and Rub

Take the image out of the water, place it face down on a smooth surface (we highly recommend using a piece of vinyl, as it keeps the image from tearing or distorting) and rub off all of the backing paper with your finger. Once you think you're done, rub it gently with a waffle wash cloth to remove remaining lint or residue.

4 Adhere the Transfer

Omni Gel is an adhesive, transfer medium and sealer all in one, so when you're ready to use your image, put some more gel on the receiving surface (In this example, a piece of sheet copper), place the image on the gel and secure and seal it with yet more gel, then let it dry completely.

Transfer Medium: The Advanced Method

This is an extremely cool method that we use sometimes when we're working with metal mesh. You'll need a tack iron, your piece of mesh cut to the size you want and a surface to iron it on. We recommend a heat-resistant craft sheet and/or a trivet that has silver on one side of it. Start with step 1 of the basic method and place your trimmed, dry image face down onto the mesh.

1 Ready, Set, Iron

Place your mesh on a heat-resistant sheet and set your 250°F (121°C) tacking iron on the image for 30 seconds per section without moving it, then iron from the middle out, taking extra care to secure the edges. A heavy hand puts more texture on the mesh, so don't be shy. When the image has transferred to the screen, you're done.

2 Take a Soak

Drop the piece in warm water or apply water to the back of the image with your fingers.

EASY DOES IT

Rewet your finger from time to time as you're rubbing off the backing paper because a dry image will tear. Rubbing with too much vigor will result in tearing also.

3 Rub and Admire

Rub away all of the backing paper and remove any residue with a waffle weave wash cloth. *Voilà!* Your image has become one with the mesh. We added a border of copper foil tape to provide smooth edges as well as a finished look.

Waterslide Decal: The Basic Method

When Lazertran first came out it didn't exactly rock our world. Hence, it sat in a drawer seemingly abandoned for a very long time. That is until I had the opportunity to converse with its designer, Mick Kelly, who opened our eyes to its vast applications on various metals. Now all we can say is "Wow! We love this product." It easily allows you to transfer and even layer images onto almost any surface imaginable. There are three kinds of Lazertran: silk, inkjet and the regular variety, which we will be using in this book. It requires taking your sized sheet of images to a copy center and having them color copy them onto the shiny side of the Lazertran sheet, using a color laser photocopier. To avoid any unnecessary confusion with the nice folks working behind the counter (we've always used Kinko's with fantastic results), tell them you want to make a T-shirt transfer and would like to use your own paper.

The method shown here is the easiest as it uses the tackiness from the back of the decal as the adhesive so no additional glue is necessary. You do not need or want a reversed print for this method.

After 24 hours, pieces that have been given a transfer with the basic method should be sealed with either an acrylic or oil-based varnish.

1 Trim and Soak
Once you've trimmed your image to size, soak the image in water for a minute or so. You will see it roll up.

2 Slide Off
Position the image on your metal (image side up) and gently slide away the backing paper that is between the metal and the front of the image.

3 Squeegee
Remove any air bubbles with your squeegee. Let the piece set for 24 hours, then you can seal it with either an oil-based or acrylic varnish to further protect it.

Waterslide Decal: The Baking Method

This is one of our absolute favorites, as it provides a beautiful, hard and permanent finish that looks as if the image and the metal are one and the same. The instructions for the oven temperature and length of baking times that we use come directly from a conversation with founder Mick Kelly, and it is our privilege to share them here with you. Pieces that have used the baking method require no further sealer, because heat sets the image.

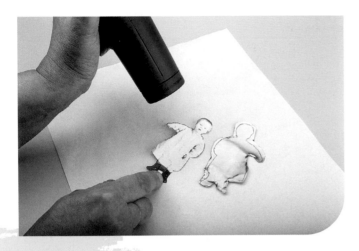

1 Prepare Your Image

With a heat gun, heat the image until you see the toners go shiny and bright; this will help eliminate any tiny unwanted air bubbles later. This quick step also ensures that the toner has completely fused to the paper.

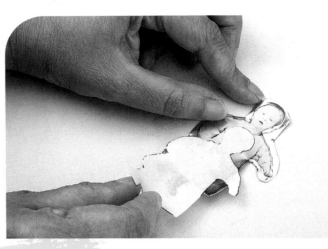

2 Face and Place

Trim your image to the size you want and soak it in water like you did for the basic method. Place your image on the metal (image side down) and remove the backing paper. Remember, your image will be reversed.

3 Wash and Squeegee

Wash off any gum residue and then use the squeegee to remove excess water and air bubbles.

4 Tray and Bake

Place on a tray and bake in your home oven on the bottom rack (a toaster oven will not work for this) at 250°F (121°C) for 10 minutes; then, very gradually over a period of up to 2 hours, increase the temperature until you reach 400° (204°C). This method requires no further sealer. (Because all ovens vary, the end result should be to have a shiny-looking surface.)

Waterslide Decal: The Ironing and Metal Foil Method

Metal foil is a wonderful material that can be purchased from most craft stores. It comes in different colors, sizes and thicknesses. Once your image has been transferred onto it, you can either stop at that point or you can emboss the metal (a technique we will cover in the next section). Very thin gauges can even be sewn on with a sewing machine. We used regular Lazertran with our metal foil, but you can use Lazertran Silk as well. Pieces that have used the ironing method require no further sealer, because heat sets the image.

WIPER-WISE

We make our own squeegees in several sizes by cutting up our old windshield wipers.

1 Place and Press
Put your image face down onto metal foil and, with your hot iron, press the back of the paper until the image has stuck to the foil.

2 Sizzle, Soak and Swish
While the metal is still hot, soak it immediately in a shallow tray of water. The backing paper should start to dislodge. Swish your hand around in the water until the backing paper floats off by itself (you do not want to pull it off).

3 Set the Colors With Heat
Take the foil out of the tray and leave it to dry. Once it has dried, you can permanently fix the colors by placing the foil on the upturned base of a warm iron.

MORE FOR YOUR MONEY

While sheets of waterslide decals won't break your piggy bank, the best and most economical way to use it is to fill up the entire sheet with as many images as possible and reserve the unused images for future projects.

BASIC METAL TECHNIQUES

35

Combining Transfer Medium and a Waterslide Decal

This variation on the metal mesh, tack iron and Omni Gel technique is done with turpentine and a Lazertran image. When using turpentine, you should work in a well-ventilated area. As with all waterslide decal methods, first trim and soak your image, then blot off any excess water.

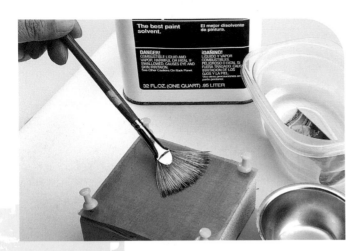

Prepare the Receiving Surface
Using an old paintbrush, brush your mesh with real turpentine (the synthetic variety will not work for this).

Remove Decal From Water
Remove the decal from the water bath and gently blot off excess water with a paper towel.

Position and Slide
Place your image on top of the mesh (image side up) and remove the backing paper.

Press
Press the image into place with your paintbrush, but be gentle. You don't need to force the image into the mesh; that will happen on its own. Add a final coat of turpentine and leave it alone for 24 hours.

A GOOD BRUSHING

If, after it's dry, there are still some areas of your image that have not merged into the mesh, another brushing with turpentine to those areas will restart the process and fix the problem.

TEXTURING AND EMBOSSING

Almost all metal can be textured and there are many ways to do it, from really simple methods and tools to not-so-simple. We've chosen techniques that you can easily do with items you probably already have on hand. Those you don't, you can easily get from your arts and crafts, hardware or general merchandise store. These include hammers, metal stamps, styluses, stencils, wood clay tools, texture plates, kitchen utensils and even a pasta machine (which can be used for roll printing with metal foil in lieu of a rolling mill). When the surface of metal has a raised design, it is said to be embossed. It's typically done on metal foil because of its thin gauge, which makes it very pliable. Various designs are achieved using the above mentioned tools and laying the foil on different mat surfaces ranging from soft (craft foam) to hard (linoleum). While true embossing is a sophisticated art form that has been used by icon-ists for centuries and has required specialized tools, it is possible to re-create similar results using simple craft tools that are readily available today.

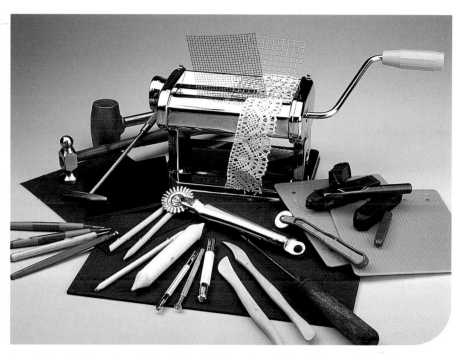

From twelve o'clock: pasta machine, craft foam (sitting under center tools), stamps, texture plates, wheels, wood clay tools, stumps, styluses, suede, cutters, work surfaces and hammers.

1 Gather a Variety of Metal Foils

Because of its thin gauge, metal foil is used in embossing. It comes in several colors. Experiment with a variety to find which you like best.

2 Emboss With a Metal Stamp

A linoleum mat is a recommended work surface, because of its density (it works best with metal stamps and chisels) but a self-healing cutting mat would also work. Set a piece of sheet metal on the linoleum. Hold the metal stamp or chisel upright and strike only once to avoid making a double impression.

3 Try Out Other Stamps

Using a chasing hammer and a linoleum mat, try giving a piece of 20-gauge sheet metal three different textures. Try using various-sized metal alphabets as well as a metal chisel.

4 Emboss With Texture Plates

Place your metal foil on a texture plate (which is its own surface and doesn't require an additional mat). We've used Fiskars texture plates, but any design with a raised relief surface would also work. Secure the foil to the plate with masking tape to keep it from shifting as you work, then rub over the foil with a paper stump.

5 Try Other Tools

A stylus, texture plates, paper stumps, stencils and a quilter's wheel can all be used to create texture in soft sheet metal. Try any other utensils or tools that you might not normally consider using with metal. For instance, metal stamps with designs that are used in leather tooling work very well with metal foils.

PAPER CRIMPERS AND TUBE WRINGERS

Paper crimpers crimp paper and tube wringers squeeze out the last remains from a tube of paint, but both of these tools also produce an interesting effect on metal (much like a crinkle-cut potato chip). The lighter-weight paper crimper, which is made of plastic and usually has aluminum rollers, should be used exclusively with metal foils. The tube wringer requires a bit more physical dexterity and is made of metal with steel rollers. It is the one to use with tin cans.

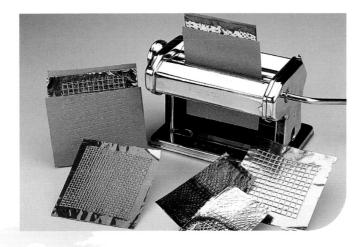

6 Drag Out Your Pasta Machine

Unless you're a clay enthusiast, you probably have a neglected pasta machine just waiting to be called into service, and this gadget works great for embossing. Sandwich a piece of lace, hardware cloth or screen between two pieces of metal foil and sandwich that between two pieces of cardboard. Run the whole package through the pasta machine. You will find you can achieve some very interesting results.

7 Add an Old and Aged Look

Once your metal is embossed or textured, you can give it a beautiful aged look by lightly applying a few drops of black fluid acrylic paint with your finger, letting it sit for a minute and then softly rubbing it off using a circular motion. Repeating this step two or three times intensifies the end result.

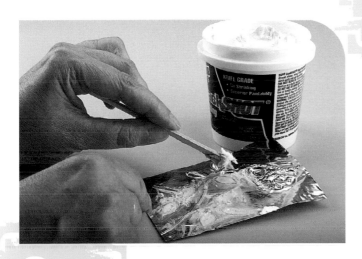

8 Stuff It

After you've embossed your design, you will want to fill the impressions to strengthen the piece. Filling safeguards it against collapsing. The filler that we've had the best success with is spackling paste (look for a variety with the words *no shrinking* on the container), which is available from the hardware store or home improvement center. Apply it to the back of the embossing with a popsicle stick and let it thoroughly dry. A little goes a long way, so buy a small container, but always check that the lid is on securely (it can easily dry up).

USING RESINS

Resin lets you take almost any hollow object, such as a bottlecap, bezel cup, small tin or shell, fill it with text, images or three-dimensional objects and view them under a transparent, hardened surface. While it may sound a bit complicated, it is quite an easy and fun material to work with. There are several different brands available, but basically they all fall into one of three categories: a one-part liquid, a powder, or a two-part variety, requiring the mixing of parts A and B (ratios will vary among manufacturers). All provide a beautiful, hard, glass-like finish that really highlights the text, images or objects embedded beneath its surface. We are fond of using all three types. Since all resins are not created equally, we will cover how and when to use each of them. We heartily encourage you to experiment to find what works best for you.

Once a resin has cured, you can drill holes in your pieces to accommodate wire, rivets or nails. This allows you to attach them, or cold-connect them, to other surfaces. If you do not wish to drill them, you can always glue them onto other surfaces.

Always allow your collage-making adhesive to dry completely before you pour the resin over it or else the adhesive will be visible in your collage. A little extra time is worth the wait. Some plastic objects may dissolve in the resin and some papers may turn transparent (if there is imagery or text on the underside of the paper, it may bleed through). Rubbing alcohol will clean up any spills as long as the resin is still wet.

Discard any leftover two-part resin; it cannot be stored once it has been mixed. For this reason, it pays to have multiple projects to coat at one time or to mix up a small batch. Resin provides a wealth of possibilities to any body of work, so experiment, play and have fun with this exciting process.

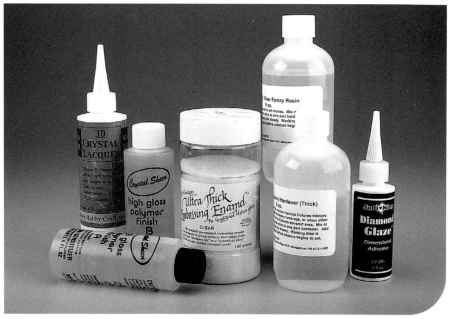

Left to right: two-part products, ultra-thick embossing powder and one-art resins.

One-Part Resin

This comes in a bottle and is the easiest resin to use. Diamond Glaze and 3-D Crystal Lacquer are two popular and similar products that dry in a few hours, but we recommend letting either cure overnight. This type of product comes with easy-to-follow package directions and should only be used in shallow containers, like the backside of an optometrist test-lens or a watch crystal.

Squeeze and Fill

Hold the bottle upright, and slowly squeeze out the resin to fill your chosen form, once your images are adhered. If your loose items shift, readjust them with a toothpick. Put a pin in the bottle opening after you use it, so that it doesn't dry out. Never shake the bottle of resin (this creates air bubbles—not a good thing, but they can be removed with a pin and some heavy breathing).

Two-Part Resin

As its name suggests, this resin comes in two parts, A and B. It is a reactive polymer compound that starts to cure to a thick glossy coating in a few hours and cures completely in 24 to 48 hours, depending on the manufacturer. There are several brand names available and the prices can greatly vary. Whichever brand you choose, carefully measure the amounts of each part as stated in the directions or the resin will not properly set (resulting in a state of eternal tackiness). Initially, the pieces must be carefully watched so that any air bubbles are dispersed before the resin sets. It's a good idea to cover the pieces with newspaper or something to protect them from floating dust particles. Place pieces on a level surface in an undisturbed area until fully cured. Occasionally some plastic objects used as collage elements may melt in the resin, so experimentation is always recommended.

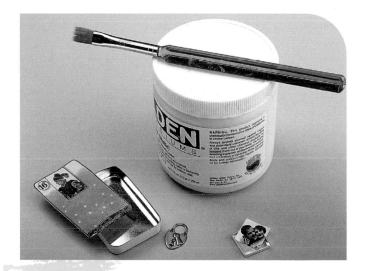

Assemble Your Collages

This is a really fun step because the sky's the limit as far as creativity and embellishment goes. Everything from text to three-dimensional objects are all fair game here. The important thing to remember is to securely glue all of the collage elements down or they will dislodge and float to the surface once you pour the resin. It's great to have lots of prepared collages on hand so that when you mix and pour your resin you will use up the entire batch instead of wasting a lot.

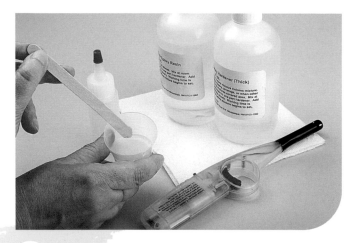

2 Mix–Mix–Mix

Working on newspaper or something that will protect your work surface, mix your resin following the package directions (this is referred to as mixing a batch). Be sure to use disposable cups and craft sticks. Stir it really well for a couple of minutes. It will look thick and a little bubbly.

3 Fill 'er Up

Put a layer of rice or sand in the bottom of a shallow container and then nest your collages in the rice. Pour the mixed resin into disposable syringes or a squeeze bottle. Fill your collage containers up to the rim with the resin, check for any air bubbles and pop them if there are any. Adjust the collages if necessary to ensure they are level in the rice.

Ultra Thick Embossing Powder

This is a large-particle resin sold in a "powder" form. When used as a bakeable resin, you want the color to be clear. Once it is baked, you can easily view the embedded objects that you've secured beneath the surface. You'll need a toaster oven for this method and not a conventional oven.

1 Embed and Secure

Once you've selected the items you wish to embed, you must first secure them. Try using tiny little balls of polymer clay (as clay was made to be baked anyway). The important thing here is to make sure all objects are securely attached before you add the resin, or they will come loose and shift during the baking process.

2 Fill

Fill the container with the ultra-thick embossing powder. It's a good idea to put masking tape around the outside edge, to prevent the powder from overflowing in the oven and creating a big mess.

3 Bake

Place your piece on a tray in the toaster oven and bake until all the powder has dissolved and the color is clear. As every oven varies, a little experimentation with the perfect baking temperature is called for here. Depending on our own oven that can be anywhere from 350°F (177°C) to broil. You do not want to over-bake it as it will burn; never leave your oven unattended.

4 Remove and Cool

When it's done, remove your piece from the oven and set it aside until cool. The end result should look like this.

SILVER LINING

Lining your oven tray with aluminum foil makes cleanup a snap.

wild and WHIMSICAL

* All work and no play—who hasn't heard that before? In today's world, we seem to have a never-ending to-do list: do this . . . finish that . . . go here . . . rush, rush, rush. Sound familiar? Maybe it's time to stop, have a cup of something, relax and hear the laughter!

In this section we will take a walk on the wild side. These first projects are filled with whimsy, nostalgia, mystery and some really cool techniques. We'll create an embellished frame complete with a faux tin type, an art doll that is created from colorful tin cans, a magnetic musical clock that really makes the *time go by*, and we'll soon reveal the secrets of Pandora's Box. Finally, we'll leave this section with a very funky family tree that will be the envy of historians and genealogists alike. Wow! I'm smiling already, and I think I feel a giggle coming on . . .

You Will Need

raw wood picture frame, 4" × 6" (10cm × 15cm) including finishing hardware

sandpaper or sanding block

clean rag

stain, acrylic paint or dye, 2 colors (for the frame)

foam brush

matte sealer

wood block

drill and ¹⁄₁₆" (1.6mm) bit, or awl

bottlecaps, 10

small nails (shorter than the frame depth)

hammer

images (to fit inside the bottlecaps)

cardstock

1" (3cm) circle punch

craft glue

Diamond Glaze, or other resin

galvanized sheet metal (to fit frame opening)

detail tin shears

image (to transfer to sheet metal)

Omni Gel

scissors

tub of warm water (for soaking)

scrap piece of vinyl

screwdriver (for attaching frame hardware)

turn buttons and screws

Domestic Goddess, Framed Portrait

Growing up in the '50s, some of my fondest recollections were of my mother cooking up a storm in the kitchen. She loved to cook, and we loved to eat—it was a match made in heaven! In this project, you will create a faux tin type, by pairing an Omni-Gel transfer with galvanized metal. The "tin type" will then be housed in a frame that is embellished with small images sealed in bottlecaps. We used one of my favorite pictures of my mom and retro food images from a vintage magazine, but feel free to use any images that speak to you and complement your piece.

Sand and Color

Even if your wood feels smooth, it's a good idea to lightly sand the frame, front and back, and then wipe off any dust with a clean rag. Add color to your frame using either acrylic paint or wood stain and a foam brush. We used transparent stain. Apply color to the front and back first, then let it dry.

Color the Edges and Seal

Once the front and back are dry, carefully paint the edges in a contrasting color. After the edges have dried, seal the frame with a matte sealer of your choice. We used a spray.

Drill the Caps

Working on a wood block, drill a 1⁄16" (1.6mm) hole In the center of each bottlecap, or punch small holes using an awl and a hammer.

Attach the Caps

Space the caps flat side down over the front of the frame. Evenly space three along the top and bottom and four along the sides. Using nails and the hammer, secure the caps to the frame.

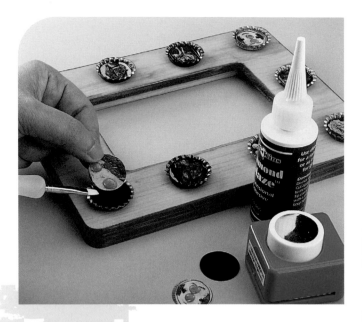

5 Select and Size

The inside of a bottlecap is about 1" (3cm) in diameter, so our tool of choice for cutting out bottlecap images is a 1" (3cm) circle punch. However you choose to trim down your images is fine, but cut plain cardstock circles the same size to back the images. This will help to conceal the nails in the bottlecaps. Glue the mounted images into the caps and seal with a resin. We used Diamond Glaze here. Refer to the section Resins, begining on page 40, for more ideas on using a resin.

6 Trim the Metal

Using your detail tin shears, cut a piece of galvanized sheet metal to fit the opening of your frame. You may need to round the corners, if your frame opening is rounded, too.

7 Apply Omni Gel to Your Image(s)

Brush Omni Gel onto your image(s) in one direction, such as vertically, using a foam brush. Let the medium dry thoroughly, then brush more medium on in a different direction (horizontally), let dry and then repeat once more in a third direction (diagonally). We like to prepare two of the same image, just to be sure we will get at least one good transfer. Refer to pages 30–31 for more information.

8 Trim and Soak

Trim the dried image with paper scissors, then let it soak in warm water for a few minutes to loosen the backing paper.

9   Remove the Paper

Lay the image face down on a piece of vinyl so that it won't shift around as you rub off the backing paper with your fingers. Remove as much of the paper as possible. After you've removed all you can with your fingers, use a waffle-weave wash cloth to gently remove the last few bits.

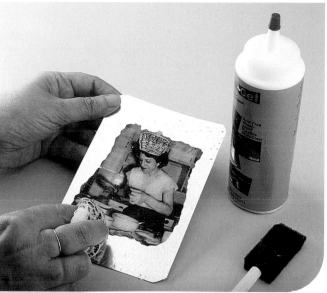

10   Adhere Your Image

Brush a bit of Omni Gel directly on the metal to act as an adhesive. Position the image on the metal then, using the Omni Gel as a sealer, brush some of the medium over the image.

11   Fit Into the Frame

Insert your sheet metal into the frame opening. To ensure a snug fit, you can fill in the remaining depth of the frame with a few layers of scrap cardboard or cardstock. The pressure used to close the clips (turn buttons) over the backing will push the metal flat. We sized a vintage game card as our last layer of backing so that our frame would look as great from the back as it does from the front.

12   Add the Hardware

Attach turn buttons to the back of your frame, using a screwdriver. The hardware should be tight enough to stay put, but not screwed in so tightly that you can't turn it. This frame came with its own dowel to allow the piece to stand up. If you wanted to hang the piece, simply add a saw tooth hanger to the back of the wood.

You Will Need

assortment of tin cans (whole cans or pieces of deconstructed tin cans)

tin snips (if deconstructing a whole can)

provided doll parts patterns (optional)

scratch paper

pencil

cardboard (for templates)

ultrafine permanent marker

detail tin shears

alcohol

face printed on fabric (made or purchased)

hand punch with ⅛" (3mm) and ³⁄₃₂" (2mm) dies

tub and tile adhesive, clear

brayer

assorted ⅛" (3mm) and ³⁄₃₂" (2mm) eyelets

steel block (or setting block)

eyelet setter

hammer

two-hole metal punch

¹⁄₁₆" (1.6mm) paper punch or Japanese hole punch

round game pieces, buttons, charms, beads or toy wheels

awl

wood block

18- or 20-gauge wire, 2' (1m)

flat-nose pliers

bone or metal charm hands

Articulated Tin Can Art Doll

Most of us grew up with dolls that were cute, traditional and conservative. Many of the dolls today, however, often referred to as art dolls, are funky, fantastic and made from a myriad of alternative materials. One such material, and one of our favorites, is the tin can—an international icon that we can all relate to. This doll is extremely simple (eyelets are the main form of connection) and a perfect first art doll project. We promise you this: Once you've made one, whatever the style, you'll definitely want to make more!

1 Gather Your Tin Assortment

Once you've selected your tins, start sketching out your doll part designs on scratch paper. After you are pleased with your parts, transfer them to cardboard, using an ultrafine marker, then trace the elements onto the flat tin can fragments. If you need help starting with a new can, see Deconstructing a Tin Can, page 14. If you'd like to re-create the same doll that we did, use the templates provided on page 53.

2 Trim Your Tin

With detail tin shears, cut out all of your doll parts and set them aside. For tips on cutting metal, see Cutting Shapes from a Metal Sheet, page 12. Alcohol will remove any remaining marker lines. Remember to take baby cuts, cut counter-clockwise and never let your blades meet.

3 Assembling the Head

There are several ways to create a doll head, but this method is one of the easiest. You'll need a piece of metal to act as the back piece and a face image that has been transferred onto fabric. Trace the cloth face onto a tin fragment and leave space for a neck, which you may or may not need. For this piece, we also left all of the flower petals on our particular tin fragment intact to extend beyond the cloth face and act as a head of hair. With your hand punch and a 3/32" (2mm) die, punch a few holes along the edge of the metal to line up with the perimeter of the cloth face. (Do not punch any holes in the cloth face yet. In a later step, you will eyelet the cloth face to the metal backing for added security.)

4 Apply the Adhesive

Remove the paper backing from the cloth head and with your fingers, evenly apply a pea-sized amount of the clear tub and tile adhesive to the back of the cloth head. Rub it in evenly, using a circular motion.

ABOUT FACE

We transferred this image onto fabric using an inkjet-ready fabric sheet from the craft store, head images from our digital clip art collection and our inkjet printer. You can also purchase premade fabric clip art sheets, where the images have already been transferred onto the fabric for you.

5 Brayer it Down

Position the fabric onto the metal head piece, brayer it down carefully but firmly and set it aside to thoroughly dry.

6 Attach the Shoulders

Now it's time to attach the body parts. This doll has an arms setup that's made from one single piece of tin and will go right behind the shoulder section of the body. The holes for both pieces can be punched at the same time. Hold the pieces together in the correct position and punch a ⅛" (3mm) hole in the center of each shoulder, where the arm comes out from the body itself.

7 Make Additional Holes

Working on a metal block, set both of the ⅛" (3mm) eyelets. Now the shoulders and arms are secured to the body. Using a two-hole metal punch, punch small holes for attaching the hands, legs and feet.

8 Attach the Head, Arms and Legs

Use eyelets to connect the body to the head. By using two eyelets, stability is guaranteed, preventing the head from flopping back and forth. Lay the head on the body until the amount of neck showing is the amount you want, then with an ultrafine marker, make two marks for the ⅛" (3mm) eyelets and punch the holes with a hand punch. Line it up and punch corresponding holes in the body, and set the eyelets. At this time you can also punch and set the rest of the body parts that will be connected with eyelets.

9 Punch the Face Holes

Using the previously punched holes at the back of the metal head piece as a guide, punch holes through the face using a ¹⁄₁₆" (1.6mm) paper punch. For holes that are harder to reach, you may need to use a Japanese hole punch.

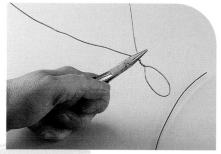

10 Mark for Hanger

Set all of the face and head holes with ³/₃₂" (2mm) eyelets. The addition of breasts will make it possible to hang up your doll without having to solder on a hanger. You can use charms, beads, game pieces or whatever—the only requirement is that they have a hole to accommodate 18- or 20-gauge wire. Place your doll on a flat surface, position the elements and mark for holes with a marker.

11 Make the Hanger

Lay your doll on a wood block, position an awl over the first marker dot and lightly hit it with a hammer. Repeat for the second hole. Remember the holes just need to be large enough to accept 18- or 20-gauge wire. Next, take about 18" (46cm) of wire, bend it in the center and make a loop. Hold the loop with flat-nose pliers and twist it three or four times.

12 Attach the Hanger

Insert the two ends of the wire through the two holes from the back of the doll. When it's pulled as far as it will go, bend the wire in the back with the loop facing up and lay the doll down flat, face up. Trim the two wires coming out of the holes to about 1" (3cm) and, using half-turns, twist the wire to act as a knot. You can also use tiny beads as an accent before you twist the wire, but it isn't mandatory.

13 Give Her a Hand

Because we're using bone hands (which cannot be hammered onto—hence, no eyelets), they must be wired on. Take 2" (5cm) of wire, spiral one end and bend it flat (see Wire, page 22). Insert the end through the back of the doll, add a bone hand, then spiral and bend the other end. Repeat for the other hand.

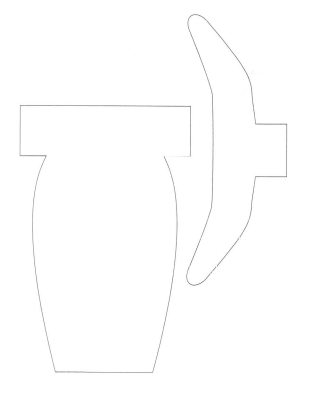

Doll template: enlarge at 150%

You Will Need

magnetic sheet

scissors

dominoes (numbers 3, 6, 9 and 12)

various images or graphics (sized to fit the box)

galvanized box

ruler

permanent marker

drill with bits the sizes of the clock and music box shafts

clock movement

music box movement

tin scrap, ½" x 7" (13mm x 18cm)

hand punch and ⅛" (3mm) die

⅛" (3mm) eyelets

steel block (or protective surface)

eyelet setter

hammer

alphabet rubber stamp set

permanent ink pad

As Time Goes By, Musical Clock

Casablanca! A story that had it all—mystery, magnetism and music. A galvanized box accepts magnets wonderfully. Using an adhesive-backed magnetic sheet to secure the time elements to the surface is a whimsical alternative to gluing or using other cold-connection options. While a timeless movie was the inspiration for our funky and musical timepiece, this is a project you'll find easy to re-create using whatever images inspire you—as they say, the fundamentals still apply.

1 Select Your Graphics and Magnetize

Cut pieces of magnetic sheet, using scissors, and adhere them to the backs of the dominoes and to the backs of all of the graphics you'll be using. You may also want to prepare an image to go over the hole that will be made for the clock shaft (we used a clock image). Our main image is actually from a popcorn tin can, but any images, including paper (with laminate on one side) or metal, would be perfect.

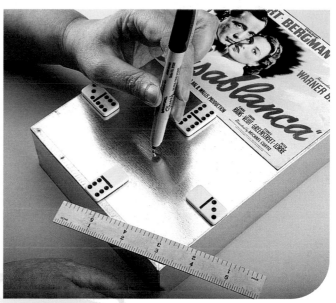

2 Mark and Drill the Center

"Stick" your images and dominoes on the box where you'd like them. Make a mark, using a permanent marker and a ruler, in the center of the clock portion. Drill a hole at the mark, just large enough to accommodate the clock shaft.

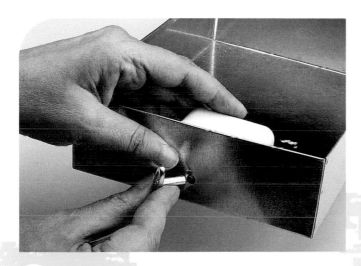

3 Drill the Music Movement Hole

Place the music box on the inside bottom of the metal box and mark where the key shaft sits. Drill a hole just large enough to accommodate the wind-up key shaft. Take the musical movement apart by unscrewing and removing the wind-up key.

4 Create the Strap

Take a piece of scrap metal (tin works well) approximately ½" × 7" (13mm × 18cm) and bend it over the top and sides of the music box, leaving about 1" (3cm) on either side. The strap will be used to hold the music box in place.

5 Secure the Movement

With a hand punch and a ⅛" (3mm) die, punch a hole in both sides of the strap. Using these holes as a guide, punch corresponding holes in the bottom of the metal box. Working on a metal block, set ⅛" (3mm) eyelets into the strap and secure it to the metal box, using an eyelet setter. Once it is secured, you can screw the wind-up key back on the shaft.

6 Embellish the Box

Rubber alphabet stamps are both fun and easy to work with. We stamped the words *play it again* on the sides of the box with a permanent ink. We also stamped the words *as time goes by* on the front. (It's also the song the music box plays when you wind up the key.)

7 Attach the Clock Movement

Insert the clock movement from the inside of the box and set the punched, magnetic image over the shaft. Attach the clock hands according to the package directions. Add a battery, wind it up and enjoy . . . here's looking at you, kid!

The Keeper of Time

This is actually a variation of two projects: the Articulated Tin Can Art Doll and this last project. This time we'll forgo the magnets, mystery and the music box movement in lieu of lots of colorful tin, eyelets, a cloth face and a crown, to create a doll that will surely keep us on time!

First, create a tin doll using the techniques from pages 51–53, but this time, use a different body style and different limbs. We made our legs from some rubber we found. Add eyelet numbers of 3, 6, 9 and 12.

Find the center of the body and drill a hole that will accommodate the clock movement shaft. Assemble the clock just like you did on the previous page, and *voilá!*

Pandora's Box, Altered Metal Purse

The lunch box—a nostalgic icon we all identify with. Most of us carried one to school and it often contained some of our favorite treats. My absolute favorite was buttered toast cut into triangles, with the crusts removed, and a thermos full of a calculated mixture of coke and milk. One dunk and I was in pure heaven! I went to Catholic school, which meant a lot of morning masses with communion and that was my lunch box breakfast of choice. While I no longer carry my lunch, I do carry a purse, so this seemed like the perfect project—a new take on an old concept.

You Will Need

plain metal lunch box

mini mint tins, 3

sanding block, disk or paper

patina kit

sealer

wood block

drill with ⅛" (3mm) and 1/16" (1.6mm) bits

assorted eyelets and brads, or miniature screws and nuts

eyelet setter

hammer

setting block

20-gauge wire

round-nose pliers

assorted embellishments

jump rings

mica powders and acrylic medium (optional)

adhesive-backed felt (for lining box and tin interiors)

1 Sand Your Tins

Working in a circular motion, sand off any graphics on the lunch box itself and the cover of the tin you'll be using as the change purse. (Sanding the graphics off of the two tins that will be on the sides is your personal choice—we left ours intact, as we wanted the graphics to remain.) Sanding provides a nice tooth for the patina to grab onto.

2 Patina the Tins

Ready-to-use patina kits are sold in all craft stores and are very easy to use. Follow the directions included on the package and, once you're satisfied with the results, seal the pieces. Combining patinas can also produce really interesting results, so don't be afraid to experiment. (See Aging Metal, pages 24–27, for more specific information.)

3 Position and Predrill the Front

Working on a wood block, drill four ⅛" (3mm) holes in the bottom of the change purse tin (near the corners) but don't attach it just yet or you won't be able to lay the box flat while you work. Also lay out and mark where the other embellishments will go and drill the holes for those as well. We're using brass chain, charms and a label holder.

PAINT OR PATINA?

If you decide to paint your box and tins, instead of using a patina, you must apply a base coat first. Gesso would be an excellent base coat choice. We would also recommend sponging on the acrylics instead of brushing them, as it provides a really unique look. Finally, be sure to seal it all well, as acrylic can chip or flake off of metal.

4 Drill the Change Purse Embellishment

We decided on a Mardi Gras coin with the image of Pandora as the embellishment for the cover of the change purse. In fact, that's how this purse got its name. Drill small holes into your chosen piece and attach it with miniature screws, washers and nuts (or eyelets or brads, depending on your preference and your piece).

5 Creating a Charm Dangle

Take about 12" (30cm) of 20-gauge wire, add a single charm on the bottom end, bend the wire with pliers and wrap it around about three times. Add more beads and/or charms, until you have a 3" (8cm) dangle. Repeat for a second dangle.

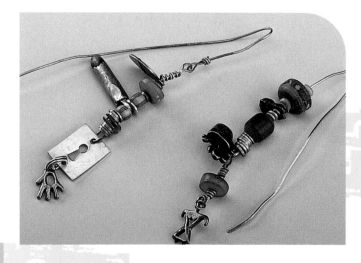

6 The Completed Dangles

Here is how your dangles should look at this point. All they need now is a loop at the top, which we'll do next.

7 Attach the Embellishments on Side 1

When the dangle is completed, make a loop about ½" (12mm) above the top bead and wrap the wire around three times and trim off any excess wire. Attach the completed dangles to the chain with jump rings. A variety of cold connections will work for attaching all of the remaining embellishments. For our box, we used brads to attach the chain and side tins to the lunch box, and the label holders were attached with eyelets. The coin on the front of the change purse was highlighted with a mixture made of gold metal powder and acrylic medium. I know you're anxious, but it's still not time to connect the change purse to the lunch box. Turn the lunch box over now, to work on the back.

Attach the Side Tins

The side tins will attach very easily with brads. Lay the box on its side, drill two ⅟₁₆" (1.6mm) holes in the side tins and two matching holes in the lunch box. Repeat this process with the tin on the other side. Now is also the perfect time to attach the change purse tin to the front of the lunch box (finally!). Be sure the tin opens from the top. Since this tin will be used more frequently, we attached it with four ⅛" (3mm) eyelets for added strength and stability.

Lay Out Your Design for Side 2

Once you've laid out your design for the other side of the box, mark and then drill all of the holes and set whatever needs to be attached with eyelets. We used brass charms, bells, tengura charms, a label holder, a milagro eye and a brass marker with the number 219, which happens to be my birthday! Once again, we attached the charms to the chain with jump rings and the chain to the lunch box with brads.

Create a Fine Interior

To give the inside of our purse and the other tins a finished look we lined all with black adhesive-backed felt. It's very easy to work with. Simply cut it to size and press it into place.

An Insider's View

The inside of the box can now look as good as the outside. Lining the box covers all of the eyelets and brads, and the look is professional and elegant.

Family Tree, Metal Collage

This family tree is a collage of sorts that honors family—specifically *my* family, in this case—and includes my parents, grandmother, aunts, uncle, special cousins and, of course, me. Instead of all the usual materials (papers, adhesive, canvas . . .) this collage is made of metal, nails and wood in a most unique and whimsical way. If geneology isn't your cup of tea, the concept of creating a collage from metal onto wood offers so many other possibilities. I'm sure you've got many ideas inside of you just waiting to grow.

You Will Need

12" × 12" (31cm × 31cm) wood board

stain, paint or dye

foam brush

scratch paper

ultrafine marker

scissors

12" × 16" (31cm × 41cm) craft metal sheet, silver, copper or brass

detail tin shears

rubber mallet

setting block

two-hole metal punch

hand punch with ⅛" (3mm) die

1" (3cm) round eyelet letters to spell *family*

⅛" (3mm) short eyelets, 6

eyelet setter

hammer

family images (to work with the circle punch)

1" (3cm) circle punch

tin fragments

nails, ½" (13mm) 18-gauge brass-plated steel

sticker maker (Xyron)

bent-nose pliers

1" (3cm) faux glass globs or Page Pebbles (Making Memories)

1 Color Your Board

The board will serve as your canvas, your background, your substrate. Whatever you choose to call it, it will need color. We used a foam brush and beautiful blue transparent stain for the front and back and a green for the edges. Paint or dye would work equally well. Once the board is colored, let it dry.

2 Design Your Tree

Taking into account the number of family members (or branch numbers) you will be including, draw a simple tree on paper. Cut the tree out and, using an ultrafine marker, trace it onto the craft metal. A template has been provided on page 64, if you wish to duplicate the tree (and number of family members) we used here.

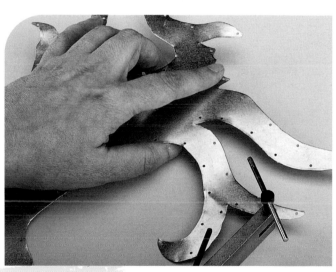

4 Make Border Holes

With the ¹⁄₁₆" (1.6mm) side of the two-hole metal punch, make holes around the perimeter of the entire tree. Keep the holes as evenly spaced as possible.

3 Trim Your Tree

Cut the tree out with your detail tin shears. As always, remember to cut slowly, counterclockwise, taking baby cuts and never letting your blades meet. After your tree is cut out, hammer all the edges with a rubber mallet, to eliminate any burrs or sharp edges, working on a setting block.

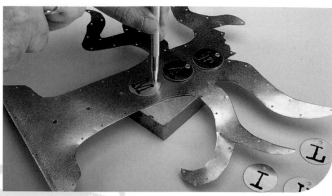

Set the Eyelets

Working on a setting block, set the eyelets into the letters.

Add the Trunk Holes

Up the center of the tree trunk and evenly spaced, punch six holes to accommodate the round eyelet letters that spell the word *family*. A hand punch and ⅛" (3mm) die work best for this.

Punch Out Images

Punch out your chosen images with a 1" (3cm) circle punch. If you turn the punch upside down, you can position the image exactly where you want it.

Tree Template: enlarge at 155%

8 Cut Out Tin Circles

Using colorful tin scraps, cut out circles a little larger than the paper images with your detail tin shears. Cut one tin circle for each paper image.

9 Create a Background

Using more colorful metal scraps, create some stars and some greenery or any other accents that may complement your family tree. Punch each piece with 1⁄16" (1.6mm) evenly spaced holes around the edges, using your two-hole punch. Little accents, like stars, only need one center hole, which you may have to drill.

10 Nail it Down

Because the nails themselves become part of the collage design, the perfect nail for a project like this should have a nice head on it and fit into the 1⁄16" (1.6mm) border holes. Also, the shaft must be smaller than the depth of the board or you'll split the wood. Using a single color of nails creates uniformity. When attaching a large piece such as the tree, begin at one end and proceed in one direction only (like from the bottom to the top. By doing this, the metal stays nice and flat and buckling is avoided. We started at the bottom and worked our way up, alternating nails on the right side, and then on the left side. Continue balancing until everything is evenly nailed down.

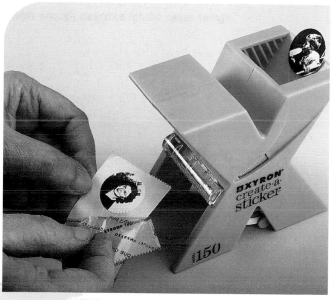

11 Create Image Stickers

One of our favorite inexpensive tools is the Xyron Sticker Maker, loaded with permanent tape. Place your images into the top of the Xyron, pull them out the bottom and then just tear them off.

Adhere Your Images

Peel the images off the backing and attach them to the metal circles that you cut out earlier. Press them firmly into place. Once they're attached, punch two holes in the edges of each metal circle, so that they can be nailed into the board. Leave enough room to attach a faux glass glob over the image but inside of the nails.

Attach the Images to the Board

Arrange the images on the tree limbs, in a manner that's pleasing to you, and nail them down. Holding the nail with bent-nose pliers makes the job a lot easier and using a rubber mallet really lessens the noise.

THE LONG AND SHORT OF IT

When layering and riveting metal, it's a good idea to have both the 1/16" (1.6mm) short and the 1/16" (1.6mm) long eyelets on hand to ensure always having the right size available.

Add Faux Glass Globs

With all of the images in place, add the fine detail images, such as our stars here, and nail them down. Lastly, just peel the Page Pebbles off the backing paper one at a time and press one firmly over each image.

Mighty Mini Tinny Mermaid

This three-dimensional sculpture is a nice change from the usual two-dimensional wall hanging and can be made from scrap wood, which you may have on hand. The nails remain the same as they did for the Family Tree, but you'll also need two longer ones for attaching the base. We used old two-by-fours and children's blocks. You'll also need gesso, acrylic paint, brushes, sealer, two hands, tin scraps, a cloth face and any embellishments of your choice.

Cut your wood to size, sand it and attach the base to the main piece of wood with the long nails. Attach the top piece of wood with two of the small nails and some glue. Gesso, paint and seal the piece, then set aside to dry.

Create a miniature mermaid doll from colorful tin can fragments. Punch border holes with a two-hole metal punch and nail it to the wood in the same manner that you nailed the Family Tree. Add a face and lots and lots of embellishments!

artful ADORNMENT

✳ The desire for adornment is a common thread that has spanned all
cultures and eras. But in the not-too-distant past, the actual creation
of jewelry seemed to be reserved for "professionals" who worked pri-
marily with gold and silver, usually in conservative ways. Recently,
however, gold and silver have had to make room for copper and
brass. The tin can, once considered to be a poor country cousin to
precious metal, now sits proudly in their midst.

This section begins with a pair of richly patinated and collaged
earrings, then moves onto a pendant that incorporates layered metal,
collage, custom findings and eyelets and includes a variation with
rivets, windows and a patina that's almost good enough to eat. Next
comes a miniature, wearable and fully functional journal made from
a tin can, then a bracelet made from found-object containers that are
collaged and filled with resin, as well as a variation piece that bakes
right in your toaster oven. This section will conclude with a beautiful
multilayered necklace made entirely from tin can fragments. It incorporates several techniques, including wire wrapping. So what are we
waiting for . . . let's create!

You Will Need

copper or brass sheet metal (22 gauge)

detail tin shears

kitchen scrubbie or sanding pad

patina of your choice (see Scrumptious Patina Recipes, pages 26–27)

matte medium/sealer

small brush

two-hole punch, or drill with ¹⁄₁₆" (1.6mm) bit

images, appropriately sized

computer-generated text (colored with an oil pencil)

chain-nose pliers

earwires (silver, niobium or base metal)

Duality Earrings

These earrings are elegant in their simplicity yet really make a strong statement. Make them for yourself or give a pair as a gift. We used copper for this project, but choose a metal and patina color that suits your individual style. Once you've made one pair, don't be surprised if you feel the need to make several more to complement every fashion ensemble.

1. Mark, Cut and Sand

Using detail tin shears, cut your chosen sheet metal to a size that pleases you, and one that you won't mind dangling from your ears. Sand the pieces well after you've trimmed them to scratch up the surface.

2. Patina and Seal

Select a patina (we used the sawdust and vinegar method, as we wanted it to have some green tones). After it has air dried well, seal the metal a couple of times with sealer.

3. Add the Holes

Using the two-hole punch, make two ¹⁄₁₆" (1.6mm) holes at one end of each piece of metal for the earwires. If you want something to dangle from the bottom, then punch holes at the opposite ends as well.

4. Add the Images

Adhere your images to the metal pieces, using matte medium/sealer.

5. Add Text

Adhere your text the same way as you did the images. If you like, you can age the white paper first with oil pencils, like we did.

6. Add your Earwires

Using chain-nose pliers, attach the earwires by opening and closing the loop at the bottom.

You Will Need

copper or brass sheet metal (22-gauge)

detail tin shears

kitchen scrubbie or sanding pad

patina of your choice (see Scrumptious Patina Recipes, pages 26–27)

matte medium/sealer

small brush

ultrafine marker

two-hole punch, or drill with ¹⁄₁₆" (1.6mm) bit

¹⁄₁₆" (1.6mm) eyelets

eyelet setter

steel block or anvil

hammer

images, appropriately sized

computer-generated text (colored with an oil pencil)

tin can fragment, 1" × 3" (3cm × 8cm)

wooden dowel or similarly-shaped object

rubber mallet

small found objects

tiny machinist screws

washers and hex nuts

nut drivers, two (optional)

Muse at Sunrise Necklace

This richly patinaed necklace is similar to the Duality Earrings, but goes a bit further by incorporating two types of connections, found objects, images, text and a hand-fashioned tin can bail. It might be fun to think of this project as a wearable collage, a complete story in miniature, based on feelings and not facts. Just let your intuition guide you and you'll create evocative pieces.

1 Mark, Cut and Sand

Using detail tin shears, cut your chosen sheet metal to a size that pleases you, and which will give you room to add images and embellishments. Sand the piece well after you've trimmed it to scratch up the surface.

2 Patina and Seal

Select a patina and apply it to your sanded metal piece. We chose the ammonia and salt patina for its beautiful blue shades. Once the metal has air dried completely, seal it a couple of times.

3 Lay Out and Mark Your Design

Gather your elements and lay out your design. Once you know where everything is going, mark where holes should be punched to attach items with wire or screws using an ultrafine marker.

4 Drill Preliminary Holes

We chose a vintage bone game piece as our side embellishment, although a small stick, metal strip or any number of other items would work equally well. As bone is a bit fragile, hammering rivets would not be a good idea, so tiny screws, washers and nuts were used instead. Two holes must be drilled in the bone (where you made the marks) with either a hand or rotary drill and a ¹⁄₁₆" (1.6mm) bit.

5 More Preliminary Holes

In the smaller of the two pieces of metal, punch a hole in each corner. The two-hole punch is perfect for this. In the larger piece, you'll notice only three holes were predrilled: one for the center-piece where the tin can bail will go, one for the bone side piece and one that lines up with the smaller metal piece. If more were drilled to start with, the pieces might not meet up properly when the rivets are set.

6 Set the First Eyelet

Working on a steel block, set the first eyelet by placing, in the following order, the eyelet on the block, the larger metal piece on the eyelet and the smaller metal piece on top of it. Insert the eyelet setter into the eyelet and set it with a hammer. One good tap is all you need.

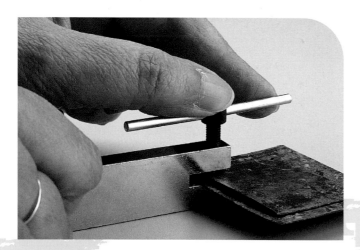

7 Set the Remaining Eyelets

Once the first eyelet is set, the rest follows easily. Hold both pieces together securely, working in the opposite corner of the first set eyelet. Place your punch right into the hole that's already in the smaller piece of metal and punch through both layers. Set that eyelet, then repeat this step until all four eyelets have been set.

8 Center the Text

Center your text and adhere it with a clear-drying medium/sealer. Here, we colored our white computer paper with an oil pencil to give the text an aged look. Add your images at this time, with clear-drying medium/sealer, as well.

BAIL MADE EASY

A bail is a jewelry finding that allows you to hang your piece on a chain. Making your own is an easy and rewarding experience. All it requires is a tin can fragment, a two-hole punch, a dowel or something similar like a knitting needle, and two eyelets. Having a few dowel sizes on hand will accommodate many chain styles.

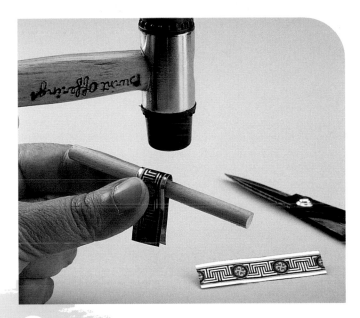

9   Create a Bail

Take the tin can fragment and trim it to a width that is pleasing to you. Then bend it over a dowel or a metal knitting needle to make a tube shape that's large enough for the chain to go through. Shape it by tapping it with a rubber mallet while it's around the dowel.

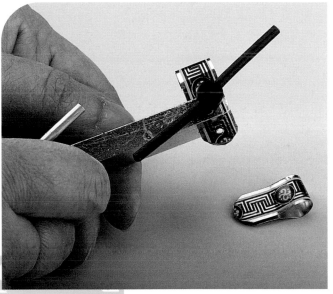

10   Punch Two Holes

Take the bail off the dowel, trim the excess and mark for two eyelet holes, one above the other. Punch them with your two-hole punch but don't set the eyelets yet.

11   Set the Bottom Eyelet Only

By setting the bottom eyelet, the bail is sort of locked into place and will be easier to work with when you're ready to attach it to your piece. With your setter on a steel block, set only the bottom eyelet. The top eyelet will connect the bail to the piece and can only be set after all the pieces have been sandwiched together. But before we set the eyelet and continue on, I would like to share something with you on the following page . . .

ELEVENTH HOUR MISHAPS AND CREATIVE ADAPTATIONS

Sometimes, for no apparent reason, something suddenly goes awry, as it did here for me, in the previous step. If you look closely at the handle of the two-hole metal punch in the previous picture, you'll notice it is **black** (which means *big* and punches a 3/32 [2.3mm] hole) and not the **silver** handle (which means *small* and punches a 1/16 [1.6mm] hole). It's always a good idea to close the side you're not working with. Simply stated, the hole I punched in step 10 is bigger than the hole I wanted or needed. While we could have edited this out, I believe it's productive to work out this problem with you, as situations like this can and will happen to all of us over time and space.

I expected to fix this by making a larger hole in the base piece of the metal and also in the tiny watch dial that was meant to be the top embellishment to be riveted to the bail, but the watch dial exploded into a bizillion irretrievable pieces as I went to punch a larger hole. There wasn't another dial to replace it with . . . so, I simply found a metal flower for a pleasing substitute, shared this mishap with you and happily moved on.

The piece will still be a powerful one, so there's been no harm, no foul. If there is a point to this, I suppose it would be that it's OK to make a mistake, or even to change your design at the eleventh hour. No design should be that rigid, and besides, don't we learn some of our best lessons from situations like this? Part of being creative means we simply adapt and move on to the next step without becoming all bogged down. So let's proceed . . .

12 Attach the Bail

Now it's time to make that sandwich. Once again working on a steel block, place in the following order the 1/16" (1.6mm) eyelet, the bail (using the top hole), the larger base piece of the metal, and last but not least, our creatively adapted, new and improved found object, on top of it all as the focal point. When it's all layered together, set the eyelet.

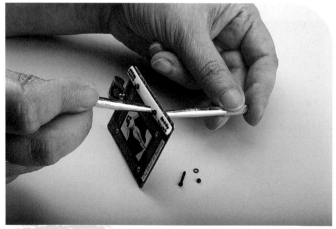

13 Attach the Bone Game Piece

Attach your first screw, washer and nut to secure the bone piece to the piece of metal. (While you can do this by hand, it works a lot better with a set of nut drivers.) After you complete the first one and it's secure, you can drill your second hole in the metal and attach the other screw, washer and nut. The hole that you drilled in the bone early on will act as a guide.

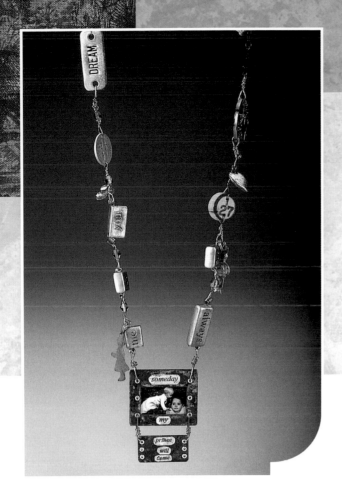

Someday My Prince Will Come

This piece features Opie and me as children. We hadn't yet met, but then, that's the beauty of "cut and paste." Here we will be cutting a window in metal without using a jeweler's saw. The materials and tools are pretty much the same as was needed for the necklace, but you'll also need a nibbler and a piece of mica. You may wish to try a new style of rivets that you haven't used yet, as well as a new patina (we used eyelets and the Potato Chip Patina on page 27). Lastly, you'll need a chain. We made ours from broken jewelry, wire and some found objects.

1 Mark the metal and drill or punch a hole large enough to accept the head of the nibbler and create a window to suit your image. Sand it with a metal file, then add a patina and seal it.

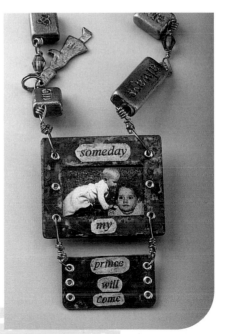

2 Create a collage that will be sandwiched between two pieces of metal, and protect it with a layer of mica. Rivet it all together and create a chain to complete the piece.

The Journal Pin

Tin can jewelry is one of our all-time favorite projects, as it elevates the tin can to more than the sum of its parts and encourages us to recycle as well. This miniature, wearable journal, made from a tin can and heavy-weight papers, is quite the conversation piece. It can also easily adapt to a pendant, if that's your preference, by turning the provided template sideways and forgoing the pinback for a chain. The interior pages may be left blank for you to record future thoughts in, or you could create artful entries in them right away to share with others who are bound to ask you, "Can I look at that?"

You Will Need

tin can fragments that speak to you

ultrafine permanent marker

journal cover template (page 81)

detail tin shears

masking tape

hand punch or drill with ⅛" (3mm) and ³⁄₃₂" (2.3mm) dies or bits

quality pinback

³⁄₃₂" (2.3mm) eyelets, 2

⅛" (3mm) eyelets (short shaft), 2

eyelet setter

setting block

hammer

cardstock or heavy-weight paper (for journal pages)

scissors

quick-coil binding punch (Bonnie's Best Tools), Japanese hole punch or ⅛" (3mm) paper punch

coil for binding

needle-nose pliers

3- or 4-ply waxed linen

beads that fit over the linen

rubber stamps and collage elements for page decoration (optional)

1 Select a Can

Either select a can and deconstruct it (see Deconstructing a Tin Can, page 14) or select a fragment from a previously deconstructed can.

2 Trace the Template

Using your permanent marker and the template provided on page 81, trace over the portions of the tin that you would like to become the front and back covers. Don't forget to trace the seven binding holes and the closure holes at the same time. Cut the two covers out, using the detail shears.

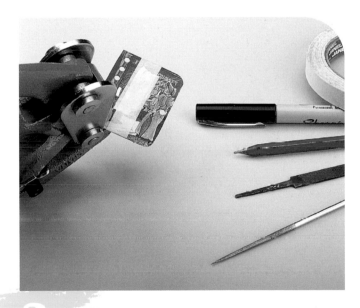

3 Tape the Covers

Align the two pieces and tape them wrong sides together. Using a ⅛" (3mm) die or drill bit, drill or punch all of the binding holes. Also punch or drill the ⅛" (3mm) closure holes on the opposite side as the binding holes and centered side to side.

RECYCLE RAPPORT

Always save unused pieces of tin, as they are wonderful for smaller projects, like jewelry and these tiny books.

TAKING THE EDGE OFF

Cleaning the holes with a round metal file will eliminate unwanted burrs and a flat file will soften the cover edges.

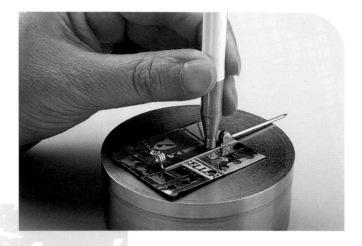

4 Attach the Pinback

Set the front cover piece aside. Center the pinback on the back cover and mark where the holes are with a permanent marker. Drill the top hole only, using a ³⁄₃₂" (2.3mm) bit (or punch with the same size die) and set the ³⁄₃₂" (2.3mm) eyelet. The part where the pin goes into the clasp should be at the bottom.

5 Drill the Bottom Hole

Now that the pinback is somewhat in place, the bottom hole must be drilled and not punched (because the pinback would interfere with the placement of the punch). Set the other eyelet.

6 Add Eyelets to the Closure Holes

Working on a setting block, set the ⅛" (3mm) eyelets into the closure holes on both the front and back covers.

7 Create the Pages

Use the same template that you used for the covers to create pages for the journal from the heavy-weight papers. There are a couple of ways to make the page holes: You can punch them with a simple ⅛" (3mm) paper punch, or you can use a coil binding system. The one used here is a quick-coil binding punch. It is a very basic model that is both easy to use and cost effective.

8 Run the Coil

Sandwich the punched pages between the covers. You're now ready to coil-bind it. Start at the bottom, insert the coil into the first hole and twist it around to continue going through all of the holes, until it comes out about ½" (13mm) above the top hole.

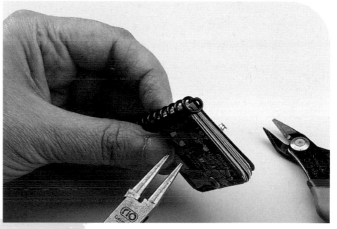

9 Snip and Crimp

Crimp the end of the coil with pliers and then reverse-twist the coil until it's only about an ⅛" (3mm) above the top of the book. Now repeat this step on the other end. You will probably have to snip off some excess amount of coil. Check to see that there's enough clearance for the pages to turn.

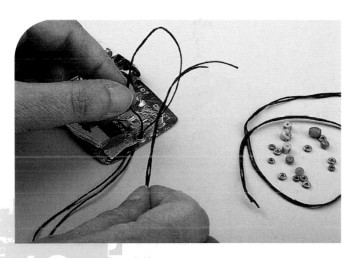

10 Add Closure

Fold about 24" (61cm) of the waxed linen in half, and put the folded end through the closure hole of the front cover. Put the loose ends through the loop and pull until taut. Make a knot. Add some beads to the linen for embellishment. Making a knot after each bead gives the closure a really nice appearance. Repeat this step for the back cover. You may now decorate the pages inside of the journal using rubber stamps and collage elements, or leave the pages blank. Tie the front and back covers together to close the journal.

Journal Cover Template: Use at 100%

Together in Time Bracelet

This bracelet was made from small vintage watch-maker tins that were collaged with papers, images and text, then filled with resin. Hardware store washers and pieces of a brass inlay strip join the containers together. A decorative clasp was made from sterling silver wire. For your own containers, you may use any hollow small-scale objects, like bottlecaps or bezel cups. The main thing is to just have fun and be creative!

You Will Need

small, empty containers

brass inlay strip, $\frac{1}{32}$" × $\frac{3}{16}$" × 36" (1mm × 5mm × 91cm)

ruler

permanent marker

cable cutters

awl or centerpunch

drill and $\frac{1}{16}$" (1.6mm) bit

two-hole metal punch

steel block or anvil

$\frac{1}{16}$" (1.5mm) short eyelets

eyelet setter

hammer

metal foil tape

collage materials

matte or gloss medium/sealer

brush

round-nose pliers

chain-nose pliers

two-part resin

tray or tub filled with rice or sand

hardware store washers or 16-gauge jump rings

newspaper

4" (10cm) of 16-gauge wire (for clasp)

chasing hammer

1 Measure Your Brass Strip

Place a hollow container on the brass strip, leaving 1" (3cm) at the end, and mark it with a permanent marker at 1" (3cm) from the other side of the container. Cut the strip with cable cutters. Repeat with the remaining containers, cutting one piece of strip for each container.

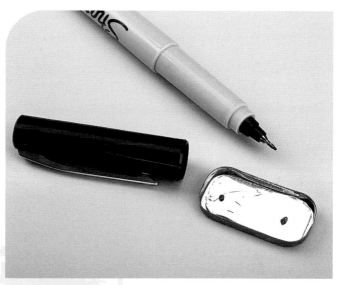

2 Make Your Mark

Using the permanent marker, mark two holes on either side of the inside of a larger container. If the container is very small, make only one mark for a single center hole.

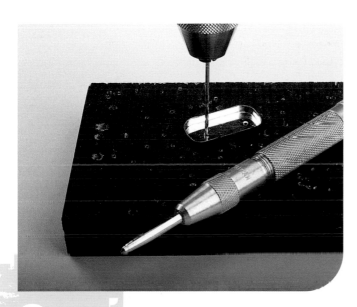

3 Indent and Drill

Using an awl or centerpunch, make indents at the marks you made. Using a ⅟₁₆" (1.6mm) drill bit, drill the holes in the container. Repeat this step on the rest of the containers.

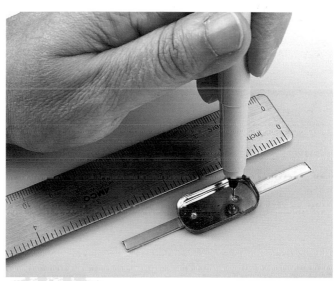

4 Place and Mark

Center a container on its brass strip, mark one hole with the permanent marker onto the strip through a drilled hole in the container. This will leave a guide mark on the brass strip. Mark one hole on each of the rest of the brass strip pieces with their corresponding containers.

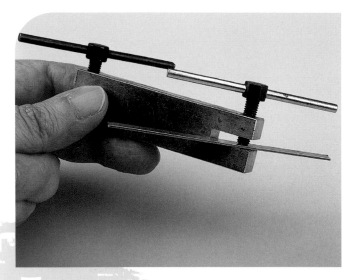

5 Punch or Drill

Use the two-hole punch (or a drill) to make the holes on all of the strip pieces. It's important to stay in the center of the brass bar or the eyelet might not go through the strip completely.

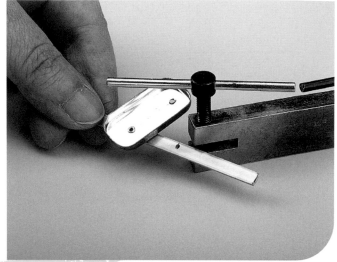

6 Set, Mark and Slide

Working on a steel block or anvil, attach the containers to their brass strips by setting eyelets into just one of the holes in each container. Mark the strips at the remaining hole with the permanent marker and then slide the containers off the brass pieces to expose the marker marks. Punch or drill those holes, again staying in the center of the brass strips.

7 Tape

Now set the remaining eyelets into each of the containers, securing them to their brass strips. Using small pieces of metal tape, tape over the eyelet holes. This will prevent the resin from leaking out through the eyelet holes.

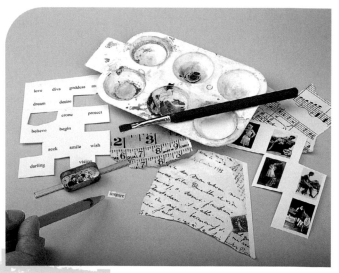

8 Collage

Using various papers and text, collage the inside of the containers using matte or gloss sealer and then apply two or three coats of the sealer to seal everything.

9 Curl the Ends

Curl the ends of the brass strips using pliers. Turn the end of the brass strip toward the container, but don't close the loop all of the way.

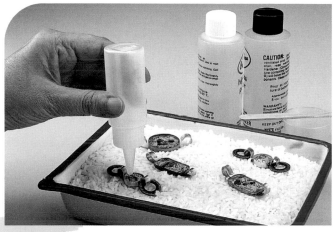

10 Mix and Pour the Resin

Set your pieces in the rice or sand-filled tray and level them as best you can. Go ahead and secure a washer to the brass strip ends on any containers that are especially small, to help weight them down and stabilize them when the resin is added. Pour in the resin. (Refer to Resins, pages 40–43, for mixing information and other details.) Cover the tray with newspaper or a cookie sheet to keep dust out of the resin while it cures. Check repeatedly for air bubbles.

11 Connect the Links

Once the resin has completely cured, add the rest of the washers to the brass strip curls and then close them with pliers.

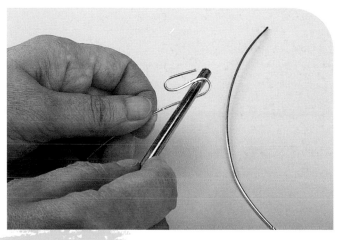

12 Create the Clasp

Begin the form of an S with the 16-gauge wire, using round-nosed pliers or anything else round as your cylinder shape (we used the end of an awl because it was the perfect size). Bend one end of the wire around the cylinder until you have a U-shape. Remove the first U-shape from the cylinder and repeat making a second U in the opposite direction. Together they will resemble an S. Snip the excess with light wire cutters.

13 Curl the Ends

Curl each end into a tiny loop, to give your clasp a very professional look.

14 Flatten

Using a chasing hammer, lay the clasp on the steel block or anvil and hammer each end (each large and small loop) until it is flat. Turn the clasp over and repeat. This strengthens the clasp and completes its "finished" look.

15 Connect

Add one end of the clasp to one of the washers on either side of the bracelet. Using your pliers, close the end around the washer as much as possible to keep it secured to the bracelet. The other end of the clasp remains open a bit, to allow you to take the bracelet on or off by hooking it onto the washer at the opposite end.

Monopoly Bracelet

The type of resin we used here differs from the two-part resin used in the Together in Time bracelet in that it is bakeable. Most materials and tools used are the same, but you will also need Monopoly game pieces and imagery, bottlecaps instead of watch tins, a toaster oven, a small amount of polymer clay and clear ultra-thick embossing powder. We used jump rings instead of washers and purchased a toggle clasp.

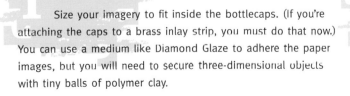

1 Size your imagery to fit inside the bottlecaps. (If you're attaching the caps to a brass inlay strip, you must do that now.) You can use a medium like Diamond Glaze to adhere the paper images, but you will need to secure three-dimensional objects with tiny balls of polymer clay.

2 Turn your toaster oven to 350°F (177°C) (oven temperatures will vary, so you may need to experiment). Fill the collaged bottlecaps with ultra-thick embossing powder and bake until the pieces melt clear. Let everything cool, then drill holes into the sides of the bottlecaps, if you didn't already attach them to a brass inlay strip (it's okay to drill through the resin, too!) Assemble the bracelet with jump rings, then add a toggle clasp of your choice to finish.

You Will Need

tin can, or tin can fragments

permanent marker

detail tin shears

rubber mallet

two-hole metal punch

¹⁄₁₆" (1.6mm) short eyelets

eyelet setter

setting block

hammer

12" (31cm) of 18-gauge wire (sterling silver or base metal)

chain-nose pliers

wire cutters

round-nosed pliers

paddle of 26-gauge wire (sterling silver or base metal)

18"–22" (46cm–56cm) of ball chain and closure (sterling or base metal)

spacer beads (sterling or base metal), 9

One Heart, Tin Can Necklace

This piece of tin was left over from a book project constructed entirely from tin cans, and the fragments were too beautiful to discard. Even though the fragments were small, they're still more than enough to construct this unique necklace, which features seven multi-layered charms. To further enhance the piece, we finished it with a sterling silver chain and closure as well as sterling spacer beads. No longer the "country cousin" to precious metal jewelry, this piece can be proudly worn anywhere.

1 Get Started

Choose either a piece of already deconstructed tin or a can to deconstruct (see Deconstructing a Tin Can, page 14) and deconstruct it.

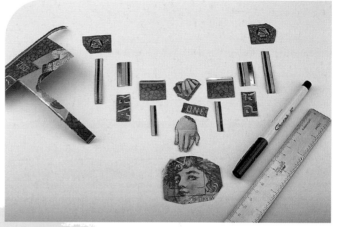

2 Rough Cut

With your permanent marker, highlight the areas you want to turn into charms. Roughly cut them out using your detail shears and lay out your design on your workspace.

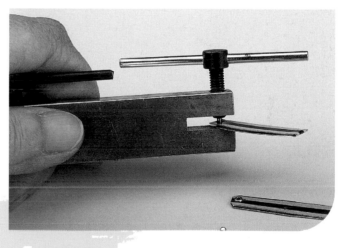

3 A Sneak Peak

Because a picture is worth a thousand words, we will jump ahead of ourselves for just a moment to view the finished charms. There are two ways to create a charm: either from a single piece of tin that gets folded over, or from two or more separate pieces. This necklace uses both. If you look back to the photo of the rough cut charms, the yellow and black stripe charm will be the example for making a single-piece charm. Look at the photo again: You'll notice there are only two red circles in the design of our tin can. I wanted to use them as the first and last charm, so they will be an example for making a two-piece charm. The centerpiece charm was made from four pieces. Once you understand the dynamics, you'll be able to effortlessly create a myriad of charms that can be incorporated into a variety of projects.

4 Begin a Single-Piece Charm

Start with a piece of tin that is long (or wide) enough to be bent in half. Once the metal is bent, flatten it with a rubber mallet. Punch a 1/16" (1.6mm) hole in the metal. This is a charm that will hang from the bottom layer or row, so whether or not you punch a second hole in the charm is your own personal choice and depends on the look you're going for. Eyelets can be used to reinforce, as well as embellish (we decided on two holes for the best aesthetics). If your charm is going to be one of those on the top layer, or row, then it must have two holes—one to connect it to the chain and one to connect it to the bottom charm. Punch the holes so that they will line up properly and center them as well.

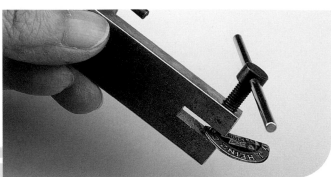

5 Trim the Charm

Once the eyelets are set, you can trim the charm with your detail shears. By doing this now and not earlier, you can be sure that the eyelet is centered and not leaning over to one side.

6 Create a Two-Piece Charm

Because I only had two circles and wanted to use them as the first and last charm, I chose to cut them in half, flatten them with a rubber mallet and back two halves to one another. Using your two-hole metal punch, punch the eyelet hole in one end only of each charm. Place the charm on your setting block and set the eyelet. Then trim the charm with your detail shears to clean up the edges.

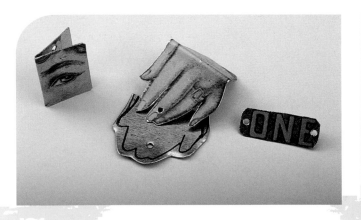

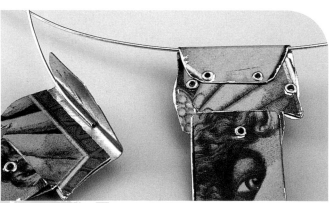

7 Begin the Center Charm

This is very much like a two-piece charm, except it has four pieces. I really liked this piece of tin and wanted to use it; a little creative manipulation made it possible. If one of your elements isn't big enough to fold directly in half, it can be riveted to a smaller piece. Here, the larger piece of the hand was joined to a smaller hand part. The face portion was wide enough to be bent sideways and it was attached with an eyelet to the middle finger of the hand. On the tin fragment itself was the word *one* and because a heart was going to dangle from this piece, we decided to call it *One Heart*. To do this, two ¹⁄₁₆" (1.6mm) holes were punched on each side of the word and it was also attached with an eyelet to the hand. A final hole was put in the bottom part of the face, so a silver heart could dangle from it.

8 Insert the Wire

If you look at the picture, you'll see that the bent part of the back of the hand hasn't been secured with an eyelet yet. This makes it easier to insert the 18-gauge wire into that groove.

CHARMING ON BOTH SIDES

Charms should always have two sides, a front and a back. This gives the charm a finished and professional look. If you don't have enough of a single piece of tin for a front and back, you could always make a back from an unrelated piece of tin, by trimming it to size and using an eyelet to secure the two pieces together.

9   The Centerpiece Wrap

Now that the wire is in place, the remaining eyelets can be set in the hand. Bend the wire into a pleasing shape and wrap one end of the wire three times around the other end. Holding the loop securely with chain-nose pliers, snip off the excess with your wire cutters.

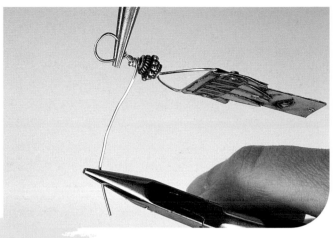

10   Drop and Twist

Drop a spacer bead down the wire (it should cover the three twists), make a loop with your round-nose pliers and hold it securely. Now with your chain-nose pliers, wrap the remaining wire around the loop three times and snip off the excess with your wire cutters.

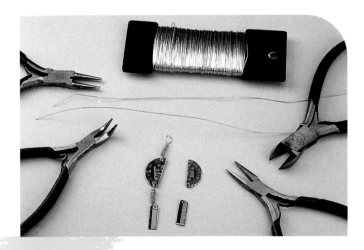

11   Wrap It Up

Shown here are an assortment of jewelry pliers: round-nose, bent and chain-nose (sometimes called flat-nose), as well as wire cutters and a paddle of 26-gauge wire. When we're not using sterling, our favorite paddle wire is bright white 26-gauge floral wire found at general merchandise stores. As a rule, you should always use two pairs of pliers when wrapping wire. But all rules have exceptions. When working with long lengths of paddle wire, which the remaining charms require, you will use your fingers until the wire becomes too short and then you'll switch to chain and/or bent-nose pliers to complete the wrap and shape the wire. The loops in the top row of charms, which will connect to the chain, are made using round-nose pliers.

12   Wrap 1, 2, 3, Twist 4, 5, 6

The key to the success of the wrap and the flow of the necklace is uniformity, and the best way to achieve it is through consistency. Each length of wire should be the same, so that the space between the top and bottom of each charm is the same as well as the space between the loop and the top charm. Start with 7" (18cm) of wire and put about 1" (3cm) through the bottom hole of the top charm. Wrap one end around the other about six times and snip off the excess. Note: Those six wraps determine the lengths of the wrap and is an amount you'll want to be consistent with.

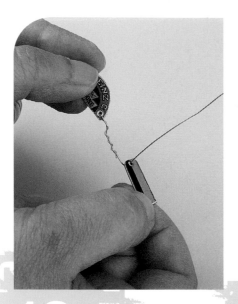

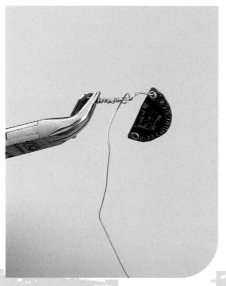

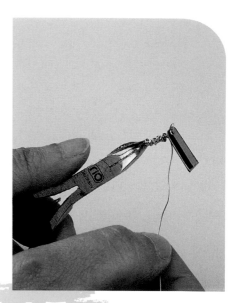

13 Connect

Place the remaining wire through the top hole of the bottom charm.

14 Wrap It Up

Starting at the bottom, wrap the wire all the way up to the top. You do not want to wrap it too tightly (you'll have no flexibility, which can cause breakage) or too loose (it will look sloppy and haphazard). With practice and patience, you will find that perfect balance that ensures successful wraps every time.

15 Wrap It Down

Now wrap it all the way back down again, remembering to keep the wrap uniform.

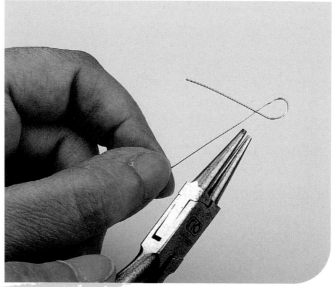

16 Straight and Narrow

Trim the excess wire. With your chain-nose pliers, shape, form and squeeze the coiled wire into a straight and narrow line.

17 Make the Connector Loop

Just like the other loop, start with a 7" (18cm) length of wire. Form a loop with your round-nose pliers and hold it securely.

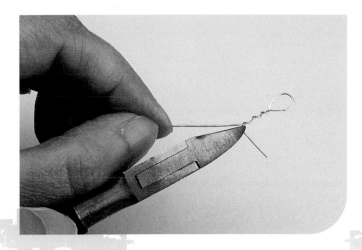

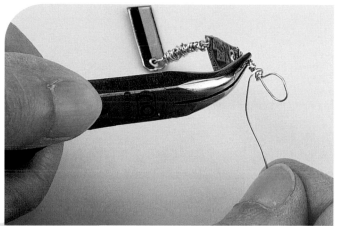

18 Twist and Snip

Wrap the shorter end around the longer end about six times and snip off the excess.

19 Wrap It Up

Insert the remaining end through the top hole of the charm. Again, wrap up one end, down the other and up again. When you're finished, trim the excess wire, then straighten, shape, form and squeeze the wrap with chain-nose pliers. Repeat this on all of the remaining charms.

20 Put It All Together

Put the center piece on the chain first (if you haven't added your heart dangle, you can do it now). Place a spacer bead on each side, then a charm on each side of the spacer, then spacers, then charms, and so on, ending with spacer beads.

21 Crimp and Complete

Not counting the center charm, which uses a thicker wire, crimp each loop of the remaining charms just a little bit. This helps keep them in place and eliminates overlapping.

kitschy KEEPSAKES

* *Kitsch* is actually a German word meaning *trash* or *junk*. As far back as the 1950s, it has been probably the most maligned, yet beloved, of cultural genres. Because much of our materials are gleaned from the detritus of society, we thought it a most appropriate name for this last section. Plus, we like the way it sounds—*kitsch*—*kitschy kitsch* . . . maybe even *sacred kitsch* . . . in any event, this is definitely not your momma's kitsch!

We'll begin with mailable art cards (which include the use of hardware cloth and baked Lazertran), then we'll move on to an artist trading card that's made from metal flashing and incorporates a patina kit. Another Fine Mesh comes next and its possibilities are seemingly endless. From there we'll explore embossing and aging metal tape as we construct a heavily embellished tin nicho, then we'll finish with a tiny keepsake tin honoring the simple pleasures in life, and offer you a final variation that includes a pewter repoussé, or embossed, heart.

You Will Need

images transferred onto regular Lazertran

scissors

craft metal sheets (we used .025 copper and galvanized flashing)

ultrafine permanent marker

detail tin shears

metal file

alcohol (for cleanup)

bowl of warm water

squeegee

baking tray

domestic or small oven (not a toaster oven)

blank notecards

hardware cloth (sometimes called hardware canvas)

tin snips

3⁄16" (5mm) hole punch for metal

cutting mat

Japanese screw punch, with 3⁄16" (5mm) tip (may be listed as 4mm)

3⁄16" (5mm) eyelets

eyelet setter

hammer

steel block or anvil

paper washers

adhesive-backed magnetic sheet (business card size)

Mailable Art Cards

We all love receiving cards (or anything from a good friend) in the mail and this one comes with its own magnetic gift attached. What an artful improvement over traditional refrigerator art! While you can choose any imagery that inspires you, using photos of family (including the four-legged members) and friends really makes a nice keepsake . . . kind of like the gift that keeps on giving.

Select an Image

Cut your chosen transferred image out with scissors. For more information on using waterslide decals (such as Lazertran), see page 33.

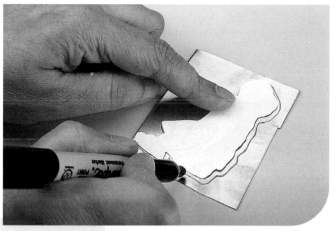

Trace Your Image

Place the image face down on your metal (we used copper but any nonferrous metal will work) and trace it with the ultrafine permanent marker.

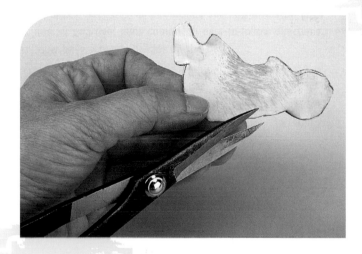

Trim and Cut

Using detail tin shears, cut out the traced image.

Clean It Up

File any sharp edges with a metal file and remove any pen marks with alcohol. When you're finished, set the metal aside.

SET THE TONE

When preparing to bake Lazertran pieces, either heat the single image with a heat gun or place the whole sheet in a medium oven for a minute to be sure the toners are fused onto the paper.

5 Soak, Slide and Bake

Place your Lazertran image into warm water. Lay the image onto the cut out piece of copper, image side down, and remove the backing paper. Blot away any excess water and be sure to wash off any gum residue, as this can turn brown during the baking process. With your squeegee and a light touch, eliminate any remaining air bubbles and smooth away any creases. Place your image on the tray and then follow the directions for The Baking Method on page 34 to complete your piece.

6 Measure and Cut Out a Window

Using your open notecard as a template, measure the hardware cloth to match the size of the card and trim it to size with tin shears. Somewhere in the center, use tin snips to cut out a window, large enough to accommodate your image.

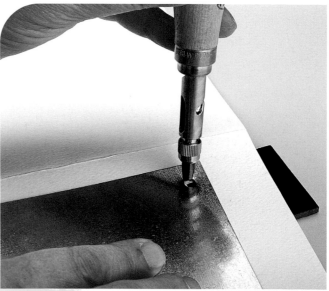

7 Insert and Mark

Cut a piece of galvanized flashing that is slightly larger than the window you just cut. Place the flashing between the card and the window. With a permanent marker, mark the four corners of the galvanized metal.

8 Punch the Holes

Punch out these four corner holes, using the Japanese screw punch. Open the card and lay it flat on a cutting mat. Place the piece of galvanized metal on the front of the card and use the corner holes as a template to punch two adjacent holes in the paper (if you punch all four holes at once, they may not line up when you're ready to set the eyelets).

Set the Eyelets

Eyelets are easily set by hand, using an eyelet setter, hammer and block, but you could also use an eyelet-setting machine. Before setting the eyelets, set a paper washer, or a regular paper reinforcer, over the shaft. This will ensure the eyelet won't come out, even with the weight of the flashing on the front. After setting the first two eyelets, punch holes for the remaining two corners, and then set those as well.

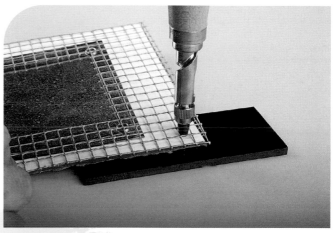

Punch the Final Holes

Close the card and set it on the cutting mat. Punch a hole (evenly spaced) in the top and bottom corners of the right side of the card (where it opens), using a Japanese screw punch. Be sure to punch through both layers of the card.

Open and Set

Open the card and set the four eyelets (two on the front and two on the back). Here, we are showing the use of an eyelet setting machine, instead of the eyelet-setting tool, which would work just as well.

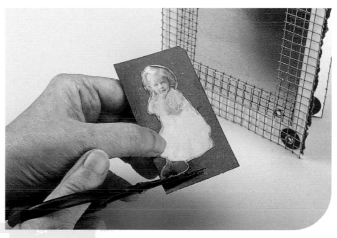

Put Her in Her Place

You can get all sorts of magnets at the craft store. Here, we're using magnetic business card backing because it is the perfect size for our "Lazertran lady." Place your image on the adhesive side of the magnet and trim to size with scissors. Position your image on the piece of flashing. Because the metal is galvanized, it will stick quite nicely and stay in place on its journey to that special person to whom you're sending this card.

You Will Need

metal flashing (or any metal that will accept patina and can be cut with tin shears)

ruler

ultrafine permanent marker

detail tin shears

antiquing and patina solutions (Modern Options)

sealer (Modern Options)

sized laser images, photos and/or computer-generated text

colored pencil (to add color to the laser copy)

favorite paper collage materials

scissors

small embellishments

two-hole metal punch

¹⁄₁₆" (1.6mm) short and long eyelets

mini eyelet setter

hammer

metal block

brush

clear-drying medium (for adhering papers)

Artist Trading Card

These miniature works of art, commonly referred to as ATCs, are created in a 2½" × 3½" (6cm × 9cm) format. They are always exchanged, never sold, and are highly collectible. Though typically made from cardstock, any material is fair game. We've developed a metal deck, to honor the people we love, which will eventually be passed on to the next generation. The card shown in this project honors my 91-year-old aunt, Frances Sartori, who passed away in June 2003. She was quite the traveler in her day and continues to inspire me. The card features one of my favorite photos of her when she was barely a woman. Perhaps you will be inspired to create a deck honoring loved ones of your own.

1 Measure, Mark and Cut

Size the metal flashing to 2½" × 3½" (6cm × 9cm), using a ruler and a permanent marker, then cut it out with your tin shears.

2 Age the Metal

To obtain the look we have here, start with a rust patina, then add green, blue or burgundy patina. Seal the patinas with sealer. (Experimentation is highly recommended—different combinations will give you different results.) For more information on applying finishes, see Oxidizing, Aging and Patinas, pages 24-27.

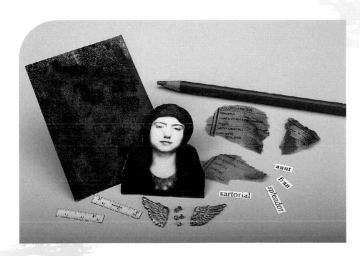

3 Gather Your Materials

This part is always such fun. Select materials that remind you of your loved one. I scanned a favorite photo of my aunt and sized it so that she would be centered on the card. Because her last name was Sartori (which translates to *tailor*), I used dressmaker's pattern paper, pieces of a tiny metal measuring tape, as well as computer-generated text. You can age your wording with a colored pencil. Add additional embellishments to suit your piece. I gave my subject brass wings, because she was, and still is, my guardian angel.

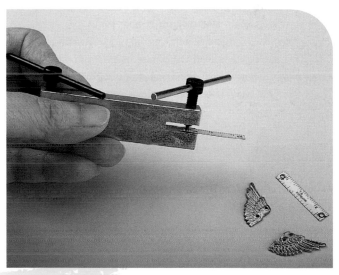

4 Punch Your Holes

If planned in advance, this project can be done entirely with your two-hole punch instead of a drill. Using the smaller ¹⁄₁₆" (1.6mm) side, punch all the holes in your metal embellishments.

Mark the Card Holes

Temporarily place your elements on the card as a guide, and mark for the holes with a permanent marker.

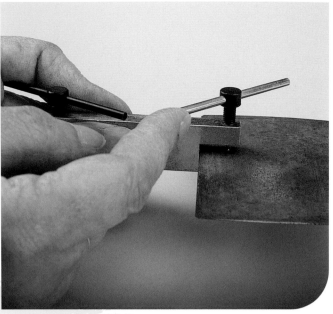

Punch the Holes

With the 1⁄16" (1.6mm) side of the two-hole punch, punch one hole at each mark.

Begin Setting the Eyelets

Working on a metal block, set eyelets to attach each metal element that will not have any collaged papers behind it. (Notice I've placed the photo back on the card, to once again act as my visual guide.)

Punch and Set Remaining Eyelets

If your metal elements have more than one hole, now that they are semisecured, mark the flashing under the remaining holes. Then, set the remaining eyelets to permanently attach the elements.

9   Secure Your Papers

Using a clear-drying medium (we recommend a matte finish, but the decision is yours), adhere any collage papers and let them dry.

10   Secure Other Elements

Secure additional metal pieces to the card with more eyelets, first punching holes in the elements and then marking and punching the card.

11   Color Your Words

Add the final focal image (here, my aunt) with more clear-drying medium.

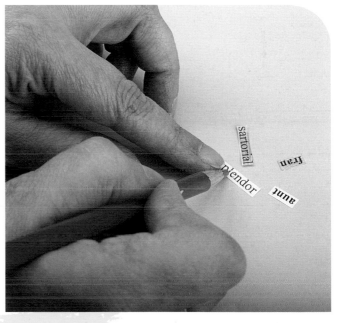

12   The Finishing Touch

Age your computer-generated words with a colored pencil. Adhere the words where you want them with the clear medium and let them dry. Congratulations—you've just started your very own ancestor deck.

Another Fine Mesh

If there was a metal that could be considered fabric, it would be woven mesh. It comes in copper, brass, bronze and steel and is soft, pliable and very versatile. You can cut it with old scissors, patina it, burn it with a mini torch or age it with liver of sulfur. In this project, you will create a dual-sided 6" × 9" (15cm × 23cm) pocketed, windowed page from the templates we've provided. Your finished piece can either be a wallhanging, a journal page or a book cover. You could even create several pages and make an entire book!

You Will Need

page, flap and pocket templates (see page 107)

copper mesh, 1 roll or package

brass mesh, 1 roll or package

ultrafine permanent marker

cork-backed metal ruler

tin shears (or old scissors)

mini torch

bone folder

¼" (6mm) copper and/or silver foil tape

liver of sulfur

small jar

cotton swabs

cutting mat

craft knife

image for both sides of the mica window

mica (or acetate), two 2½" × 2½" (6cm × 6cm) pieces

Japanese hole punch, with ⅛" (3mm) die

⅛" (3mm) eyelets

washers, ⅛" (3mm) hole

eyelet-setting tool (or machine)

setting block

hammer

images for both sides of each slide mount (4 total)

slide mounts, 2

regular brads, 8 (plus a few extras)

text (any kind—we used a label-making machine)

embellishments (you can never have too many)

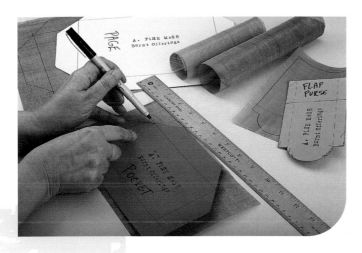

1 Cut, Size and Trace

Copy the templates for the page, flap and pocket from page 107. The flap will require two pieces of brass mesh for stability. The page itself is copper, and the pocket should be brass. Place each template on its appropriate color of mesh and, using an ultrafine marker and a corkback metal ruler, trace the templates. Rough-cut each piece of mesh about 1" (3cm) out from the traced line, to make fine trimming easier. At the end of each dotted line, make a tiny mark on the mesh (inside of the shape), as this will aid you when you're ready to make the folds.

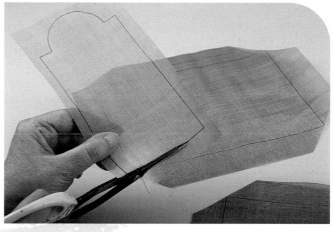

2 Cut Them Out

With tin shears or old scissors dedicated to projects like this, cut out the mesh pieces along their outside lines. You'll end up with one page, one pocket and two flaps.

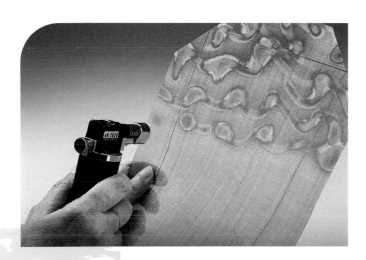

3 Torch Them

Hold one end of the mesh and, using a mini torch and a back and forth motion, torch each piece of mesh. Be careful, as the mesh will become hot! (See page 25, Aging With a Mini Torch, for more information.) Torch the brass pieces as well.

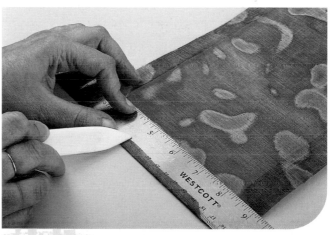

4 Crease Three Sides, Then the Top

Place the copper page down on your work surface and crease the two sides and the bottom by placing the ruler on the marker lines and scoring along the line with a bone folder. When both sides and the bottom are creased and folded, turn the page over. Again, with a ruler and bone folder, crease and fold the top line.

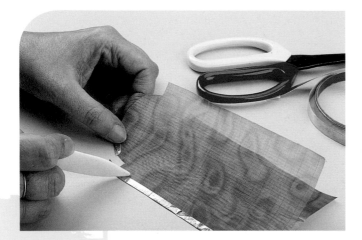

Prepare the Flap

Place the two trimmed flap pieces together and secure them to each other with foil tape, centering the tape over the edge of the mesh and folding it over on either side. Burnish the tape well with your bone folder. You can use copper or silver foil tape in a 3/16" (5mm) or 1/4" (6mm) width. We've found it easier to work with the wider width. Stained glass supply stores and rubber stamp stores both carry foil tape.

Age the Tape

Mix up a small batch of liver of sulfur, following the package directions, and pour it into a jar. Age the foil by dipping a cotton swab into liver of sulfur and dabbing it onto the tape, until you achieve the desired results.

Begin the Mesh Window

In the upper third of the page, place the window template on the mesh and trace it using an ultrafine marker and a metal ruler. Draw an X from corner to corner, then draw a smaller box inside of the larger box. This will provide you with a seam that will be folded over later on, and the marker line will show where you'll cut.

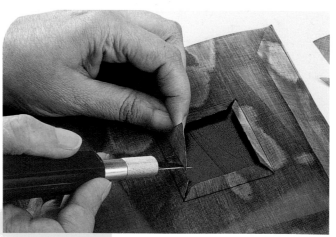

Cut the X

Place a cutting mat under the window you've just drawn and, with a craft knife, cut the X corner to corner in the larger box. Fold the pieces back to the lines in the smaller box and cut them off. You're left with four seam pieces.

9 Crease the Seams

Again, using the metal ruler and a bone folder, crease and fold the four seams.

10 Create the Mica Window

Sandwich your images between the two pieces of mica and edge with foil tape like you did for the flap piece. (You can age the tape with liver of sulfur if desired.)

11 Punch Eyelet Holes in the Window

Working on a cutting mat, punch a ⅛" (3mm) hole in each corner of the window. (A Japanese hole punch is our hole-making tool of choice for this project, as it goes through the mesh, mica, foil and paper like butter, but other punches will also work.)

12 Set Eyelets in the Mesh

Working on the cutting mat place the mica window over the window in the mesh and using the mica as a template, punch four corresponding holes into the mesh. Add a washer to each side of the holes, and insert the eyelets. Set the eyelets, using an eyelet setter on a setting block.

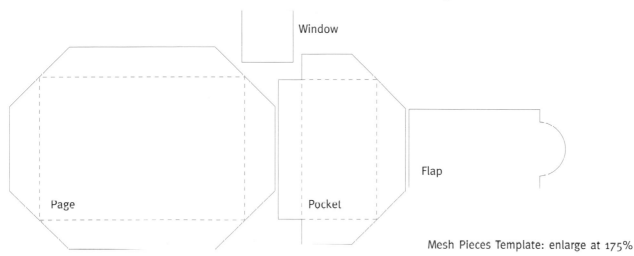

Window

Page

Pocket

Flap

Mesh Pieces Template: enlarge at 175%

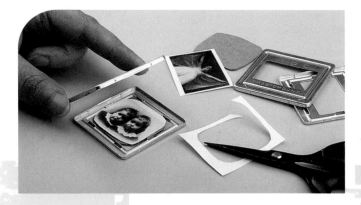

13   Insert Your Images

Trim your images to fit inside the slide mounts, set them inside and snap them together. You'll need one mount for the flap and another one for the pocket.

WHAT IS MICA?

If you're not familiar with mica, it's a mineral that is sold in craft stores and comes in several sizes, from small tiles to large sheets. It is totally heat resistant and relatively transparent, making it a wonderful material for creating windows. If your mica piece is very thick you can split it in half with your finger nail by sliding it between the layers and gently pulling it apart. In fact, one piece of mica can be split several times over, providing you with several thinner layers.

14   Set the Holes

Punch holes in the corners of your slide mounts. Use brads to secure one slide mount to the flap and the other to the pocket. Punch and set the eyelets and washers around the edge of the flap spaced about an 1½" (4cm) apart. Punch the edge holes in the mesh page and in the pocket, spacing them about an 1½" (4cm) apart. Line up the holes in the mesh pocket to the page holes and set all the remaining eyelets and washers on both sides and the bottom of the page. Once the pocket is attached and the eyelets and washers are set, turn the page over.

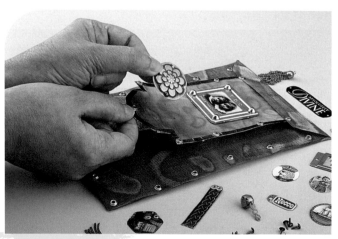

16   Embellish, Embellish, Embellish

There are no rights or wrongs here, as embellishments are a matter of personal taste and will differ with each individual. We attached ours with wire and brads and used an assortment of both vintage and contemporary findings, as well as tin can fragments. We also used a label maker for some of the words on one of the slide mounts, but any type of text, including computer-generated, would work as well. Lastly, we made a shrink plastic charm for the inside of the pocket.

15   Attach the Flap

Insert the flap under the front page seam and, working on a setting block, attach the flap to the page seam using eyelets and washers.

I Can See Clearly

You, too, will see clearly through this delicate and transparent page. All tools and materials that you used for Another Fine Mesh will be needed here, and you will also need a transparency sheet, an image to go behind it, a colorful sheet of paper and embellishments, embellishments and more embellishments.

1 Sandwich your image between a colorful sheet of paper and a transparency sheet that has a subtle design. Ours has foreign script, but you can purchase other versions or print your own with an inkjet printer.

2 Once you've prepared your "sandwich," place it on the inside of your copper mesh page (the side that has the flaps) and secure it together with eyelets. Decorate the backside and the front with embellishments.

Guardian, Tin Nicho Shrine

Tin nichos are very popular throughout the Southwest and have a distinictive style all their own. This nicho is fashioned from a single piece of metal, and the top is folded in a style intrinsic to the tinsmiths of New Mexico. We've included a template for your personal use. The angel itself is hand drawn, traced and embossed on metal tape.

You Will Need

nicho template (see page 115)

spray adhesive

craft metal sheet, silver-colored (22 or 24 gauge)

brayer

detail tin shears

cutting mat

ruler

hand-held glass cutter

setting block

center punch tool

latex or rubber gloves (optional)

waxed or freezer paper

adhesive release agent (like Goo-Gone)

rags (for the adhesive release agent)

metal hand punch

¼" and ⅛" (6mm and 3mm) dies

¼" (6mm) eyelets, 6

eyelet-setting tool

bottlecap and pull tab from a soda can

red enamel paint

small brush

wood block

rotary or hand drill

⅛" and ¹⁄₁₆" (3mm and 1.6mm) bits

pop rivet gun (and 1 rivet)

hammer

copy of angel drawing (see page 115)

3" (8cm) wide aluminum tape

cardboard

masking tape

stylus with a small tip

black fluid acrylic

cheesecloth

1¼" (3cm) wide copper slug/snail barrier tape

alphabet eyelets (to spell *guardian*)

permanent marker

lathing strips that have been stained or colored, and cut to ⅞" × 4¼" (2cm × 11cm), 2 pieces

C-clamp

milagros or charms, 6

miniature screws, nuts and washers, 6

nut driver tools, 2

light flush cutters

small metal file

image for inside the bottlecap

1" (3cm) circle punch (optional)

clear-drying adhesive

Adhere to the Metal

With either spray adhesive or a Zyron machine, adhere the copied template (from page 115) to the metal. Use a brayer to ensure good adhesion.

Cut the Metal

With tin shears, trim the metal around the template. As always, cut slowly and counterclockwise, taking baby cuts, and try to avoid letting your blades meet.

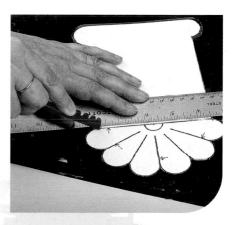

Score the Metal

Lay the metal on the cutting mat and place your metal ruler a little under the line you want to score (to compensate for the width of the glass cutter) and, with the glass cutter, score only the lines marked with an arrow. (A little elbow grease is necessary for this step!)

Center Punch the Circle

Place the tin on a setting block and make a small indent at the dot in the center of the circle, using a center punch tool.

Score the Back Lines

Turn the metal sheet over, template side down. Working on a mat, score the lines to the left and right of the center line (the same way you did on the front side), using the center-punched dot and the points where the scallops meet as a guide.

6 Squirt, Squish, Lift and Discard

Lay the metal on waxed or freezer paper. Squirt a generous amount of adhesive release on the paper and rub it in with your fingers, covering the entire area. (You may wish to wear rubber gloves to do this.) Let it completely soak in. Lift off the paper, throw it away and clean the metal with a cloth.

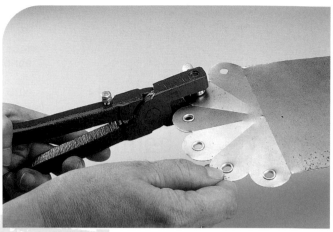

7 Punch the Top Holes and Set the Eyelets

Mark the center of each scallop with a permanent marker and punch a hole at each mark, using a hand punch with a ¼" (6mm) die. Because the eyelets are large, we are using a hand-held setting tool instead of a setter, hammer and block. There are as many eyelet tools as there are eyelets, all designed to make your task easier.

8 Punch and Paint

With a hand punch and a ⅛" (3mm) die, punch a hole in the center of the bottlecap and the solid part of the pull tab (this will serve as a hanger). Color the inside of the bottlecap with red enamel paint, using a small brush, and set it aside to dry.

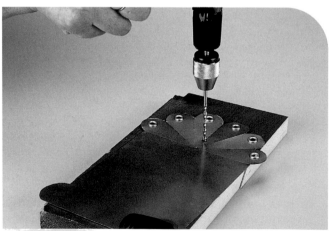

9 Drill the Circle

Working with the metal on a wood block, drill a hole at the center punch mark made earlier, using a ⅛" (3mm) bit.

10 Pop Goes the Rivet

Sandwich the bottlecap on the front, the metal in the middle and the pull tab on the back. Insert a rivet through the bottlecap side, tip pointing up, and place the rivet gun over the rivet tip, applying pressure to the "sandwich" as you squeeze one or two times, until it "pops." (For a refresher, see Pop Rivets on page 19, and all pop rivet guns come with easy-to-follow directions.) You now have a handy hanger on the back.

11 Emboss With the Stylus

Make a copy of the angel drawing (you might want to make an extra, in case you need it) and cut a piece of aluminum tape a little larger than the image. Layer the copy over the aluminum tape, and secure both pieces to a piece of cardboard with masking tape. After everything is securely taped down, trace the angel, using medium pressure and a stylus that has a small tip. Once the angel is completely transferred to the metal tape, discard the paper and work directly on the aluminum tape to go over any angel lines that did not transfer well.

12 Age the Angel

Cover the embossed angel with black fluid acrylic. You can use your fingers to rub it into the grooves if you like, then let it set for a bit, but not long enough for the paint to dry altogether.

13 Buff Up the Color

Using cheesecloth and rubbing gently in a circular motion, wipe off most of the fluid acrylic. (For best results, this step should be repeated a couple of times, until the desired results are achieved.) Once you're satisfied, set the angel aside until later.

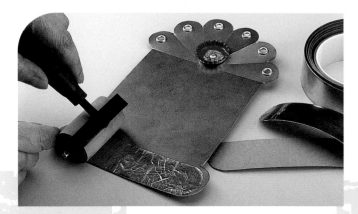

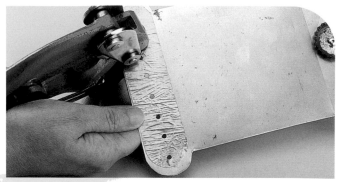

14 Apply the Copper Barrier Tape

Because of its size, copper slug and snail barrier tape is perfect for many applications. You can get it online or from hardware stores (in states that have slugs and snails). Cut a piece slightly smaller than the bottom portion of the nicho (make a template if you wish) and round the edges. Adhere it to the nicho with a brayer.

15 Punch the Letter Eyelet Holes

Using a permanent marker, place a dot for each letter you want to punch a hole for onto the copper barrier tape. Then, with a hand punch and a ⅛" (3mm) die, punch the holes.

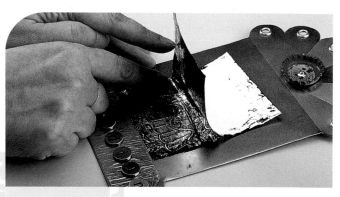

17 Adhere the Angel

Position the angel over the metal and carefully adhere the end that the adhesive is exposed on, using your fingers. Slowly roll down the angel, pulling off the remainder of the backing as you go. Don't rush—do a little bit at a time until it's on completely.

16 Remove the Backing

Working on a setting block, set the eyelets. Try not to strike them too hard until you have them positioned so that they read in a straight line. Carefully begin removing the backing from the embossed angel tape. Start at the bottom and expose about 1" (3cm).

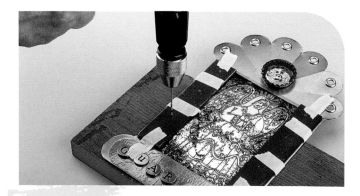

NUTS FOR NUT DRIVERS

Nut drivers are tiny tools designed to tighten miniature screws. They are sold where the screws are sold. If you use two drivers, you can have one on the back and one on the front—just insert one in each side and turn. *Voilá!*

18 Drill the Wood Holes

Tape the colored wood lath strips to the nicho with masking tape. Clamp the piece to a wood block with the C-clamp and drill ¹⁄₁₆" (1.6mm) holes at the top, center and bottom of each piece.

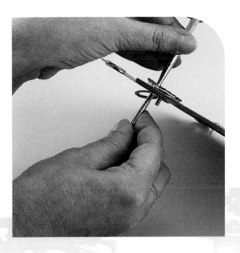
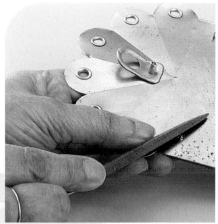

19   Attach Milagros

Attach milagros (charms) to the nicho. Insert screws through the milagros holes on the front (it will go through the wood, the metal and come out the back). Add a washer and then a nut and tighten with nut drivers.

20   Snip and File

If your screws are too long to be flush with the end of the nut, snip off the excess with flush cutters and file them with a metal file.

21   Add the Image to the Cap

The inside of a bottlecap is about 1" (3cm) in diameter, so a 1" (3cm) circle paper punch works nicely to punch out the image you wish to place inside the bottlecap. Use any image that speaks to you. To stay thematic, we rubber stamped an image using permanent ink onto aluminum tape and punched it out. You may wish to create a cardboard washer to compensate for the added height created by the pop rivet. Add a small amount of clear-drying adhesive (we used Diamond Glaze) to the inside of the bottlecap, place the washer down in it, and then place your image on top of the washer (if you stamp an image on metal tape like we did, you must remove the backing tape before you place it on the washer) and press it into place. Set it aside to thoroughly dry.

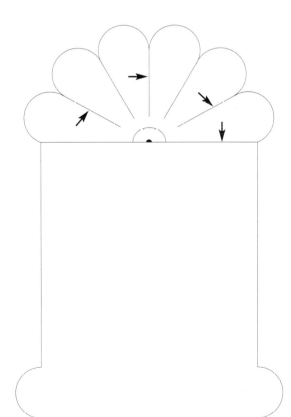

Nicho & Angel Templates: enlarge at 150%

Simple Pleasures, Keepsake Tin

Small tins and intimate spaces seem to go hand in hand. Ready-to-use tins are easy to recycle with a little TLC. Add your creative touch, a bit of ephemera that tells a story, and soon you'll have created a beautiful memory. The tin in this project is 4½" × 5" × ¾" (11cm × 13cm × 19mm) but any small tin would work equally well. (Think of all of those Internet provider tins you regularly receive.) Our tin tells the story of Aunt Louise's journey from childhood to womanhood. From diaper pins to garters, all is revealed!

You Will Need

small tin

assortment of ephemera and embellishments related to the tin's theme

ultrafine permanent marker

two-hole metal punch

eyelets, ¹⁄₁₆" and ⅛" (1.6mm and 3mm), mixture of short and long

eyelet washers, ⅛" (3mm)

eyelet setters, ¹⁄₁₆" and ⅛" (1.6mm and 3mm)

setting block

hammer

wood block

drill with ¹⁄₁₆" and ⅛" (1.6mm and 3mm) bits

hand punch with ⅛" (3mm) die (optional)

two pieces of cardstock

scissors

adhesive of choice (Xyron machine recommended)

thin wire and/or waxed linen

eyelet phrase

needle tool

brads

rubber-stamped phrase on cardstock (optional)

brass frame and/or a slide mount (to frame your photo)

paper punches, ¹⁄₁₆" and ⅛" (1.6mm and 3mm)

word washer (Making Memories)

1 Lay Out Your Cover Elements

Assemble the elements you want to have on the front of the tin. Then, once you've decided on your layout, using an ultrafine marker, mark where you will need holes to go, to secure the embellishments. These holes can be for eyelets or brads.

2 Punch Holes in the Embellishments

With the 1/16" (1.6mm) side of the two-hole metal punch, punch whatever holes you can in the embellishments. You'll want to attach some elements to each other before you attach anything to the tin, so do not punch any holes in the tin just yet. I punched the brass corner piece, the rusted metal vine and the four corners of the brass frame.

3 Drill the Holes in the Tin

Set eyelets in any of the elements that you wish to be secured together before they are actually attached to the tin. In this case, I secured the copper "crown" to my tin type with small copper eyelets to make it easier to secure the two to the tin in one piece. Working on a wood block, drill whatever holes in the tin that you're ready for now, with a 1/16" (1.6mm) drill bit. Here we drilled one corner for the top of the frame and only the top hole for the rusted vine.

Create Holes for the Final Elements

Place the cover of the tin on a setting block and set the first two eyelets, then continue drilling and setting until all of your elements that use eyelets are secured to the cover. Here, all that remain for the cover are a ⅛" (3mm) hole in the bottom of the tin for the eyelet phrase and a smaller hole in the top for a brad. The eyelet phrase and the brad will eventually attach to the inside of the tin, over the cardstock, providing extra holding stability for the cardstock. The bottom hole was made with a hand punch and a ⅛" (3mm) die. A hole was made for the brad with a drill and a ¹⁄₁₆" (1.6mm) bit.

Punch the Cardstock

Using the eyelet phrase hole and the brad hole in the tin as a template, mark the cardstock and punch corresponding holes with a ⅛" and a ¹⁄₁₆" (3mm and 1.6mm) paper punch.

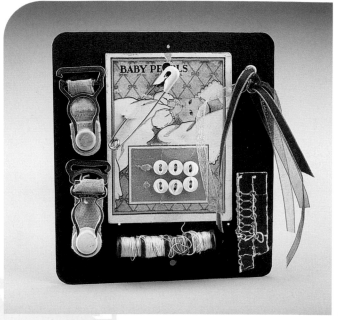

Attach Ephemera to Cardstock

Cut and size a piece of cardstock to fit inside of the left half of the tin. Run the cardstock through the Xyron machine but leave the backing paper on. Arrange ephemera over the cardstock. Attach all of your pieces to the cardstock using thin wire, or eyelets and eyelet washers. When using the wire to attach items, you can either punch holes to sew through with a needle tool, or you can use a hand-held punch.

Peel Off the Paper

Peel away the backing paper, using a needle tool to help peel up the paper in hard to reach places that have wire and eyelets over it.

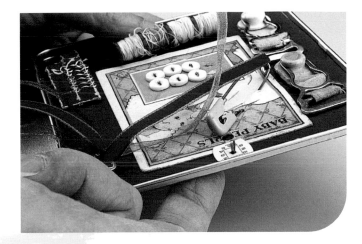

8 Adhere the Phrase and Brad

Press the cardstock into the inside of the tin and insert a brad into the hole we made on the front of the tin. If it's snug, use a needle tool to loosen up the opening. The tips of the brad reminded me of the hands on a clock, so I added a tiny watch face to the inside of the tin and now the brad has become a design element. Lay the phrase face down on a setting block and set the tin cover side down over the eyelet shaft. Set the eyelet, along with an eyelet washer. (Remember to check that it's straight before you hit it with all of your strength.)

9 Cover the Eyelet Hole

For aesthetics' sake, if you'd like to cover the eyelet phrase hole on the inside, rubber stamp a phrase on a scrap of cardstock in a corresponding color and adhere it over the eyelet hole with any type of adhesive.

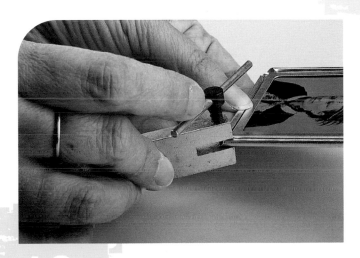

10 Punch the Slide Mount

Place your image into the slide mount and punch one $\frac{1}{16}$" (1.6mm) hole in each corner. Our mount is metal, so we're using a two-hole metal punch. If your mount is paper, then a paper punch will do the job.

11 Mark the Holes

Run the remaining piece of cardstock (after it has been cut to fit inside the other side of the tin), through the Xyron. Again, leave on the backing paper. Lay out your design and, using your ephemera as a guide, mark where the 1/16" (1.6mm) holes for the slide mount will go with an ultrafine marker. At the same time, mark holes for the other embellishments. A 1/8" (3mm) hole will be needed at the center top and the center bottom for another eyelet phrase and for a washer phrase.

12 Drill the Final Holes

With paper punches, punch the marked holes in the cardstock. Secure the elements that required 1/16" (1.6mm) holes (with the exception of the slide mount) using brads or eyelets (remember to use paper washers at the back of the cardstock to secure eyelets). Peel off the backing paper and adhere the cardstock to the inside of the tin. Place the tin on a wood block and drill the 1/8" (3mm) holes for the eyelet word and the large word washer.

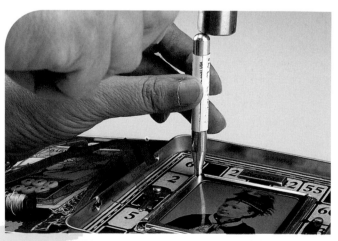

13 Set the Larger Eyelets

Working on a setting block set those eyelets. The washer requires a 1/8" (3mm) long eyelet that should be inserted from the back to create a sandwich in this order: eyelet, tiny copper washer, keepsake tin, word washer and a final tiny copper washer.

14 Set the Mount

With an ultrafine marker, mark and drill the holes for the slide mount eyelets. Using 1/16" (1.6mm) long eyelets (they need to be long to attach to the tin) and working on a setting block, set the eyelets one at a time.

My Heart Belongs to Daddy

This variation has lots of metal embossing, including the words *my* and *daddy,* as well as the heart. In addition to the usual eyelets, brads, collage elements, papers and aging materials, you will need metal foil (we used pewter), a hard mat, a craft foam sheet, embossing tools, a paper stump, nonshrink spackle, a heart image, metal paint, an optomotrist lens and printed letters to use as a template for both words.

1 Working on a hard mat surface and a soft craft foam sheet, draw a heart (or trace one), using an ultrafine permanent marker, on the metal foil. Working on a linoleum mat or cutting mat, emboss the image using various stylus tips and work the design from both sides until you get the result you like. Age the metal with black fluid acrylic and add any collage elements that you would like to use.

2 To emboss the words, secure words printed on paper to a piece of metal foil. Turn over and start embossing with a paper stump and finish with a stylus. (You should be able to see the letters through the paper.) When you're done, fill in all of the impressions with spackle and adhere additional embellishments with eyelets and brads.

Gallery

Whole 9 Yards

This bracelet pairs tin charms, etched copper charms and found materials with sterling silver.

Cousins

These earrings have nibbler-cut windows, a collage sandwiched between mica and sterling silver charm dangles.

Tin Can Art Dolls

The larger doll features multiple techniques combined with a lot of found object embellishments. The smaller doll has been scaled down to jewelry size and made into a pin.

Que Sera Sera

This is a musical doll assemblage whose head is a vintage metal food chopper. The inside of her body is a smaller collaged box with vintage game pieces from Go to the Head of the Class. It plays *Que Sera Sera*.

La Mer

The housing of this music box assemblage is a found wood box embellished with tin fragments. The top features parts from a vintage erector set, a Greek octopus can with metal bezel cups, glass cabochons and metal eyelet letters. The *La Mer* sheet music was added to the inside of the box with Lazertran. It plays the tune *La Mer*.

Rich and Ripe

This gourd and mixed media sculpture features a face from scraps of metal we found on our beach, including the mouth which is part of a brass hose nozzle. A Pre-Columbian tin calendar makes up the headpiece.

The Java-Bot

A four foot sculpture, the head for this piece is a vintage train embellished with a plumbing knob. The mouth is a funnel and the body a tin coffee can.

Gallery

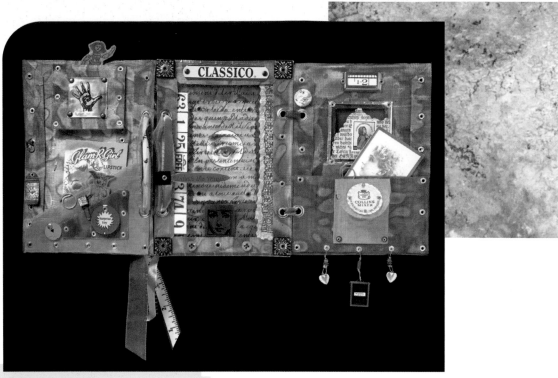

All Bound Up
This book is completely made from metal mesh and is bound with an assortment of ribbons.

Circus Book
The front and back covers are riveted tin and aluminum. The pages are paper, leather and mesh and are embellished with circus ephemera.

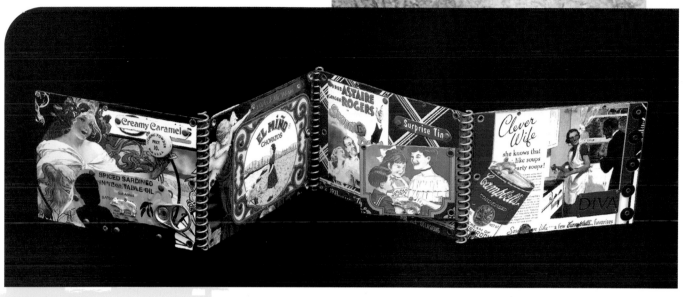

Clever Wife

This book is made entirely from an assortment of metals: mostly tin cans enhanced with copper and aluminum flashing, riveted together and embellished with silver milagros. The coil binding features custom copper hinges.

Day of the Dead

Made from a hardshelled gourd, this book's pages are made from the gourd's pulp. The front features a tiny tin nicho shrine, with a riveted window copper piece, which houses a tin skeleton.

Resources

The materials used for the projects in this book should all be available from either a hardware store, a stamp store or an arts and crafts store. If, however, you have trouble locating one or more particular items, consult the sources listed here for purchasing and retail information.

ONLINE RESOURCES

www.artchixstudio.com
clip art, embellishments, transparencies and rubber stamps

www.bearingbeads.com
clip art and rubber stamps

www.burntofferings.com
tin shears, mini eyelet setter, two-hole metal punch, nibblers, clip art, Omni Gel, rubber stamps and copper mesh

www.coffeebreakdesign.com
eyelets, setting tools and embellishments

www.collageartist.com
rubber stamps

www.copicmarkers.com
markers

www.docmartins.com
metal paints and markers

www.harborfreight.com
hand-held punch sets, general metalworking tools

www.lazertran.com
Lazertran

www.micromark.com
miniature screws, nut drivers, general metalworking tools

www.modernoptions.com
patina kits

www.riogrande.com
jewelry findings, tools, oxidizers, patinas, metal sheet

www.stampersanonymous.com
rubber stamps

www.stampsalad.com
Rubi Coil Binding Machines

www.teeshamoore.com
clip art and rubber stamps

www.tuscanrose.com
clip art and CD's

www.zettiology.com
rubber stamps

INSPIRING METAL AND MIXED-MEDIA ARTISTS

www.ninabagley.com
Nina Bagley

www.michaeldemeng.com
Michael DeMeng

Bobby Hansson
author of The Fine Art of the Tin Can (Sterling Publishing, 2005)

www.bearingbeads.com
Beckah Krahula

www.susanlenartkazmar.net
Susan Lenart-Kazmar

www.lobue-art.com
Keith Lobue

FURTHER LEARNING

Art retreats and workshops are a wonderful way to explore, expand and connect with kindred souls as well as your creative muse.

Artfest
Hosted by art guru's Teesha and Tracy Moore annually in Port Townsend, Washington
www.teeshamoore.com

Art Continuum
Hosted annually by Ginny Carter in Cleveland, Ohio
www.stampersanonymous.com

Art & Soul
Hosted by Glenny Densem-Moir annually in several locations.
www.artandsoulretreat.com

Artiology
Hosted by Nikki Charles annually in Atlantic City, New Jersey
www.artiology.com

The Hacienda Mosaico
A beautiful artist retreat in Puerto Vallarta, Mexico hosted year round by Sandra "Sam" Leonard
www.haciendamosaico.com

Index

DISCOVER EVEN MORE creative ideas with these North Light Books!

ART TO WEAR
BY JANA EWY

There's no better way to show off your creative talents than to adorn yourself, your family and friends with your own works of art. Whatever your unique style, this book shows you how to create jewelry, accessories and clothing that match your personality. Author Jana Ewy demonstrates how to dress up jackets, sweaters, t-shirts, flip-flops, purses and belts with paint, ink, metal, fabric, fibers, beads and even Chinese coins. You'll be inspired to make your mark on your clothing and accessories by the over 25 projects and variations included in the book.

ISBN 1-58180-597-7   paperback 96 pages   33110

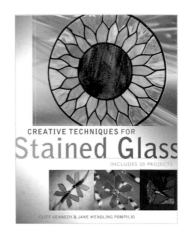

CREATIVE TECHNIQUES FOR STAINED GLASS
BY CLIFF KENNEDY & JANE WENDLING POMPILIO

Inside *Creative Techniques for Stained Glass*, you'll find 25 projects that combine stained glass techniques with the latest trends in bead, wire and metal crafting. The projects are in a range of styles, from traditional to contemporary— you're bound to find projects that match your style perfectly. Best of all, the projects are simple to construct. The book provides easy-to-use templates and step-by-step instruction. With a wide variety of projects, including light switches, lamps, window panels, suncatchers and purses, you'll have trouble choosing which one to start first!

ISBN 1-58180-604-3   paperback 128 pages 33162

BEAD ON A WIRE
BY SHARILYN MILLER

In her latest book, magazine editor and popular author Sharilyn Miller shows crafters of all levels how to get in on the popularity of jewelry and beading. Inside *Bead on a Wire*, you'll find an in-depth section on design and construction techniques that make it a snap to get started. You'll love to make the 20 step-by-step bead and wire jewelry projects, including gorgeous earrings, necklaces, brooches and bracelets. You'll be amazed at how easy it is to start making fashionable jewelry that's guaranteed to inspire compliments.

ISBN 1-58180-650-7   paperback 128 pages 33239

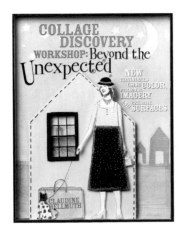

COLLAGE DISCOVERY WORKSHOP: BEYOND THE UNEXPECTED
BY CLAUDINE HELLMUTH

In a follow-up to her first workshop book, Claudine Hellmuth taps into a whole new level of creativity in *Beyond the Unexpected*. Inside you'll find original artwork and inventive ideas that show you how to personalize your own collage pieces using new techniques and interesting surfaces. In addition, the Collage Challenge, compiled by Claudine and other top collage artists will spark your imagination. Whether you're a beginner or a collage veteran, you'll enjoy this lovely book both as inspiration and as a practical guide.

ISBN 1-58180-535-7   paperback 128 pages 33267

These and other fine North Light titles are available from your local art and craft retailer, bookstore or online supplier.